Karma, Mind, and
Quest for Happiness

Karma, Mind, and Quest for Happiness

•◈•

The Concrete and Accurate Science of Infinite Truth

Dr. Susmit Kumar

iUniverse, Inc.
Bloomington

Karma, Mind, and Quest for Happiness
The Concrete and Accurate Science of Infinite Truth

iUniverse books may be ordered through booksellers or by contacting:

iUniverse
1663 Liberty Drive
Bloomington, IN 47403
www.iuniverse.com
1-800-Authors (1-800-288-4677)

ISBN: 978-1-4697-5022-4 (sc)
ISBN: 978-1-4697-5025-5 (hc)
ISBN: 978-1-4697-5024-8 (e)

Library of Congress Control Number: 2012901941

Printed in the United States of America

iUniverse rev. date: 01/25/2012

Dedicated to Baba

Contents

Acknowledgments ix

1. Introduction 1

2. Happiness—A State of Mind 7

3. Belief. 11

4. Science, Spirituality, and Religion 15

5. Brain and Science 27

6. Mind, Tantra, and Mantra. 35

7. Karma and Potential Energy 61

Endnotes. 83

Acknowledgments

•◆•

For thirty years in India, I was very close to Shrii Shrii Anandamurti ji, a great spiritual person and the founder of Ananda Marga. Ananda Marga is a global spiritual organization with centers in more than one hundred countries. He was from my mother's hometown, Jamalpur, a small city in Bihar state of India. I and my family were privileged to witness several of his actions that cannot be explained by present-day science. Our science is just two hundred to three hundred years old, whereas our universe is billions of years old. And our science may not have knowledge about tens of thousands of scientific laws of our universe: that is, Mother Nature. Great spiritual persons know something about the workings of the Universe that are not common knowledge right now, and that's why we claim their actions to be "miracles," "magic," or religious dogma, according to our individual frame of reference. Having a PhD in science, I have tried to explain in this book some of those actions.

I take pleasure in acknowledging the generous help of Trond Overland in editing this book; Garda Ghista, Firdaus Ghista, Professor

Raj N. Singh and Professor Raj Bhatnagar of University of Cincinnati, Cincinnati and Dr. Ram S. Singh of Cincinnati for their helpful discussions in writing this book. I am always thankful to my PhD advisor, Professor Stewart K. Kurtz of Pennsylvania State University, who taught me how to do research and also how to write a research paper/article. I would like to thank General Secretary of Ananda Marga Pracaraka Samgha for allowing me to quote extensively from various books of Shrii Shrii Anandamurti ji. Above all, I am grateful to my mother, who inspired and guided me in more ways than I can ever say.

1

 ⋅—◆—⋅

INTRODUCTION

When the Indian Air Force patrolled the Andaman Islands after the 2004 tsunami, they wanted to find out about the condition of the aboriginal inhabitants. Having had very little contact with the outside world, the islanders started shooting arrows at the helicopters, thinking they were birds. The universe is billions of years old, whereas the history of mankind on planet Earth goes back only a few ten thousands of years. In the whole wide field of spirituality, we relatively inexperienced human beings are no different from the aboriginal inhabitants of the Andaman Islands.

Humans in their present form can be traced back two hundred thousand years. Human civilization can be traced back ten thousand to fifteen thousand years. Our science and technology have made exponential progress during the last couple of centuries. This relatively newfound technology has drastically reduced communication time between the various continents. In the nineteenth century, it used to take months to travel from Europe to North America; today, it takes only a few hours and in the near future, perhaps only a few minutes. On the other hand, our technological advancements have also increased how we think of distance and time exponentially. Until recently, people used to consider units of time and distance in terms of hundreds of years and miles. Now, astronomers measure time in billions of years and distance in trillions of miles. Still, science has discovered the scientific laws of only 4 percent of the materials in the universe. The remaining 96 percent is politely labeled as "dark matter' and "dark energy," as no one has been able to "see" it yet.

From this scientific point of view, our modern knowledge about the universe is still scarce. What we do know is that the universe is ancient and that our knowledge about it is constantly changing. As recently as the seventeenth century, the great Italian scientist Galileo Galilei, who revolutionized astronomy by developing the telescope, was persecuted for claiming Earth revolves around the sun, which was contradictory to the Church's belief at the time. After the publication of his book *Dialogue Concerning the Two Chief World Systems* in 1632, he was tried by the Inquisition, found, "vehemently suspect of heresy," and forced to recant. He had to spend the rest of his life under house arrest.

The exponential growth in scientific knowledge is leading a large number of people to question their religious beliefs, or even reject them altogether. Some of those religious teachings are, at most, a little over two thousand years old; some are a thousand years older. There is no doubt the founders of these religions were significant personalities in their time. Nevertheless, like any solid scientific theory, a spiritual theory also needs to be free from the distorting influences of time and place.

I have had the opportunity to experience both Eastern and Western cultures. Prior to arriving in the United States in 1989, I spent my first thirty years in India. Apart from being in contact with two great spiritual personalities in India, I had the opportunity to read biographies of numerous spiritual persons and works on spirituality. In my view, great persons like Christ, Buddha, Moses, Prophet Muhammad, and Krishna knew something about the workings of the universe that were not common knowledge, and that's why we claim their actions to be out of the ordinary, or even part of religious dogma. The fact is we simply do not know how to explain the stories about them. Mental or spiritual science may someday show that none of our characterizations are correct and that these teachers were applying deep scientific principles in everyday life.

During the last ten thousand years, many saints in Asia have explored the human mind and its relationship with the Infinite. Most of them did it after first establishing the limitations of physical pleasure and intellectual knowledge. These saints got wonderful results. When Newton saw an apple fall from a tree, he came up with the famous Newton's Laws of Motion. Similarly, when saints started to explore the functioning of their minds and how everything around them was created, they developed a theory called Tantra. In this book, I try to explain scientifically certain facts of Tantric philosophy, such as the constituent parts of the mind, the effect of mantra on the mind, and how karma may be scientifically defined and explained. We shall also see how Tantra is free from the distorting influences of time and place.

ARRANGEMENT OF CHAPTERS

In chapter 2, "Happiness—A State of Mind," I discuss happiness as a state of mind. Worldly objects like wealth, sex, and power are sources of happiness, but they are not ultimate goals. Moreover, such worldly pleasures are not absolute but relative in nature.

In chapter 3, "Belief," I show how dogma is not a proper base for belief. Instead, we need to learn to keep our minds open.

In chapter 4, "Science, Spirituality, and Religion," I explore the fact that although science has progressed exponentially during the last two hundred to three hundred years, there are still perhaps thousands or even millions of scientific laws of Mother Nature (our universe) that remain undiscovered.

In chapter 5, "Brain and Science," I examine the parts and functions of the human brain and how they differ from those of developed animals. I also discuss some recent technological advances in the study of the brain and their practical uses.

In chapter 6, "Mind, Tantra, and Mantra," I go into Newton's experience of observing an apple falling from a tree, which produced his famous Laws of Motion. I show the similarity between this event and those experienced by the saints of Asia, who explored the human mind and its relationship with the Infinite about ten thousand years ago. Based on their own experiences, these saints established the limitations of physical pleasure and intellectual knowledge and came up with miraculous scientific results and the wonderful theory called Tantra. This chapter also contains an explanation of the three constituent parts of the human mind and how it differs from that of plants and animals. Chakras (or cakras) and their propensities will also be explained, as well as how the systematic chanting of a mantra affects the human mind, the significance of Aum, and the types of food one eats and their effects on the mind.

Chapter 7, "Karma and Potential Energy," explains how each and every second (in inhaling, exhaling, walking, talking, etc.) affect us and the possibility we inadvertently apply hundreds (maybe thousands of) subtle scientific laws of the universe every day. Five hundred years ago, nobody thought that chemical, electrical, or nuclear energy existed. Most likely, human beings will continue to conceptualize and discover myriad energies and their scientific laws. In order to explain physical phenomena, science came up with these energy terminologies. Similarly, I explain how "karma" is also an energy term, similar to "potential energy." I also explain how karma and the laws of the universe play a role in life after death.

2

.•◆•.

HAPPINESS—A STATE OF MIND

Much as we try to obtain happiness, we do not get the desired result every time. In most cases, the results are not according to our wishes, and this causes unhappiness or sorrow. It is said that even love causes unhappiness: either the wife or the husband has to die first, and this will cause unhappiness to the one who survives.

Two recognized schools of philosophy are idealism and materialism. Lord Krishna's doctrine of action is an example of the first: one should work according to capacity and should not worry about the results. In the *Bhagavad Gita*, Lord Krishna says, "*Karmanye waadhikare astu ma phale su kadachana,*" or, "Surrender the fruits of actions unto Me." This is one extreme. Buddhism also represents this philosophy. Here, the ideal is detachment from worldly objects. The other extreme type of philosophy is the materialistic, or capitalist, attitude: that is, to indulge in worldly objects or pleasures.

Both positions are flawed. It is impossible to detach oneself completely from worldly objects. Unless one has some goal—that is, to achieve some desired pleasure—he or she cannot work with maximum effort. Hence, it is very difficult to follow the verse in the Gita. On the other hand, as already stated, results achieved are often not what one wants, and this causes pain or sorrow.

Pain, sorrow, and unhappiness are inevitable in the world, so how can they be minimized? Personally, I am completely against Buddhist philosophy, which is to detach oneself from all worldly objects in order to eliminate unhappiness. The follower of this principle will not enjoy any pleasure in life.

Longing after an object may also not bring happiness. In the movies, when the camera is focused on a single person's face, that person's face is very clear, while those of others are hazy. Similarly, if we focus our mind on a particular object, that object controls our passion, and other things become less important. I try to work with all my abilities to get the best results, but if I do not get the desired results, I focus my mind on some other object to minimize the unhappiness. Even so, I had to experience unhappiness first.

We may also try to rationalize our unhappiness by playing down the importance of our desired object. Suppose I am to take an exam. I study very hard. If I get the desired results, everything is okay. If the results are not according to my wishes, I may think, *This is not going to be of any importance to me after twenty years, so why should I bother with this?*

There are people who claim money is everything in life, and everything can be gotten with money. Yes, money is an important factor in life, but it is not everything. Everyone always has a list of worries. If an item is removed from this list, another takes its place. People who do not have enough money generally place money at the top of this, along with other worries. Wealthy people may have something else on the top of this list. Items that often occur in this list are money, illness (his own or his close relatives), job search, search for a better job (if you already have a job), and relationship issues (at home or at work). Michael Jackson was very famous and had a lot of money, but he could not sleep without the help of his doctor. Catherine Zeta-Jones, the actress, has biopolar II disorder. Rich and famous people are frequent visitors to rehab clinics. Obviously, financial wealth is not the answer to all of life's problems.

Happiness is a state of mind. Worldly objects like wealth, sex, and power are sources of happiness, but these are not ultimate goals. Such worldly pleasures are not absolute but relative in nature. A graduate student assistantship in the United States brings in about $13,000 per year. The assistant compares him- or herself with the professor, whose salary is around $60,000 per year, and thinks if only he or she had that much money, life would be very easy and full of happiness. But after a few years, when the student finishes his or her degree and earns $60,000 per year in some corporation, her or she starts comparing himself with someone whose salary is higher and feels bad once again.

Wealth, power, and so on are all relative in nature. There will always be others ahead in the queue. A better philosophy for happiness is: I will try my best to achieve a goal, but whether I achieve that goal or not, I will always think of life's long-term meaning in order to minimize losses or pain. I do not have control over the results of most of my actions, and hence, there is no point in thinking about the actions or the results as I cannot change the outcome.

One should never look back. One should look ahead, because we cannot change what has already happened. One should always try to see the bright side of everything. Start comparing yourself with those who are behind you in the queue. After all, it could be they are better off than you are.

In order to negotiate a curve, the outer wheel of a car has to travel more than the inner wheel; otherwise, the car will have an accident. Every car and truck has a differential, which makes sure the outer wheels do just that while negotiating a curve. This is how functional relationships work.

3

• ◆ •

BELIEF

To begin with, I would like to ask readers a question (I hope Apollo astronauts are not among them): why, if you have not gone to the moon, do you believe men ever walked on it? Most probably, readers will answer that they learned about it through the media. In other words, the belief that moon landings actually took place is due to acceptance of what was seen on TV: the live transmissions of Apollo astronauts from the moon.

One could, of course, argue that the United States made an artificial surface to resemble that of the moon somewhere—say, in the Arizona desert—and televised a landing there to the world. To try to satisfy persons who argue along this line, you may show them moon rocks, which were brought back by the Apollo astronauts, and photographs and films of the landing. But the authenticity of all your evidence may still be questioned. In fact, whatever you show to aboriginals living in remote parts of Australia will not make them believe the landing ever took place.

Immediately after 2004 Indian Ocean tsunami, the Indian Air Force went to help people in some of the Andaman and Nicobar Islands in the Bay of Bengal. On some of those islands, there are tribes still living in the Stone Age and do not know about modern science. When they saw the helicopters sent to help them, they simply shot arrows at the helicopters.

The point I am making here concerns belief. We have belief in modern technology, and that's why we accept that the moon landing and other space flights actually took place.

Suppose you are walking with your friend, who tells you that a passerby is a Nobel Prize winner in physics and is very knowledgeable in the field. Would you believe it? If you have faith in your friend, you may. But if you do not have faith in your friend—or in anyone for that matter—how can you verify the passerby is as good in physics to warrant receiving a Nobel Prize? You will have to learn physics, and only then will you be able to plumb the depths of his or her knowledge. Without knowledge of physics, however, you have no right to doubt the person's expertise.

This is true in the case of spirituality, too. Most of us have no knowledge in this area. But because of the opinion we hold about ourselves, we may think we have general authority in numerous fields, including spirituality, without having any in-depth knowledge in those fields.

Spirituality and Miracles

Spirituality is often equated with miracles. The great saint Vivekananda opined, however, that people should not blindly believe stories about miracles. He said it is possible for everyone to experience them. We may call incidents miracles because modern science is only two hundred to three hundred years old and is not yet able to explain them. Of course, in order to experience miracles, an ordinary person shall have to meditate or follow the paths set by spiritual leaders.

One should not consider spirituality and religion to be the same. In my opinion, spirituality is much more scientific than is religion and 99 percent practical. Physics, chemistry, biology, and so on are, say, 50 percent practical and 50 percent theoretical. By doing mental exercises and using appropriate Sanskrit mantras, one can come to know much more about these so-called miracles. I also put forward that not all stories about miracles are accurate. Some are, of course, while some cause harm to spirituality.

No living body has seen God. The concept, or mere feeling of God, proposes there is always somebody watching me or is there to help me—especially in the time of need. Hence, the feeling or concept of God is much more powerful than what a toddler feels when near his or her mother. For this reason, a person who believes in God tends to be more psychologically strong and satisfied than a nonbeliever. On the other hand, problems arise if a group of people starts to claim their God is better than the God of others. Everyone thinks his or her parents are the best. But the moment one thinks his or her parents are the best and all others are bad, we have a problem.

4

．◆．

SCIENCE, SPIRITUALITY, AND RELIGION

Science and Our Universe

Most world religions are two thousand years old or less. Our universe is billions of years old. Until two hundred to three hundred years ago, people used to consider time in terms of hundreds of years and space in terms of the nearby village, city, or country. About six hundred years ago, America was not yet discovered. The exponential growth of scientific knowledge during the last two centuries has undermined central scriptural claims. Today, we know human beings roamed the planet as far back as two hundred thousand years ago. The Hubble space telescope, launched into space by NASA in 1990 and located about 375 miles above Earth's surface, captures light that was emitted billions of years ago and has traveled trillions of miles. The Chandra telescope, launched in 1999 by NASA, does the same job by capturing X-rays in space. Millions and billions of planets like ours dot the universe, and humanlike creatures may exist on several of them.

According to a study by Australian astronomers, there are 70 sextillion (7 followed by 22 zeroes), or 70,000 million million million, stars. They said there were likely many million more stars in the universe, but the 70 sextillion figure was the number visible within range of modern telescopes.[1] According to one estimate, there are about 300 billion stars and at least 50 billion planets in our Milky Way. Out of these 50 billion planets, life could exist on at least 500 million of these planets.[2] According to Alan Boss of the Carnegie Institution in Washington, D.C., there could be one hundred billion trillion (1 followed by 23 zeroes) Earth-like planets in the universe, making it "inevitable" that extraterrestrial life exists.[3] According to some scientists, it is possible to travel faster than light, which, if true, would enable humans to travel to stars in few days.[4]

According to the Greek philosopher and scientist Aristotle, the universe had an infinite past. His statement conflicted with the theory of some religions that God created the universe in an instant. In 1931, Georges Lemaitre, a Belgian Catholic priest and scientist, proposed the big bang theory for the origin of the universe. According to the big bang theory, our universe originated from an extremely hot and dense state at some time in past (about 14 billion years ago) and has continued to expand to this day. Figure 4.1 shows some facts about our universe.

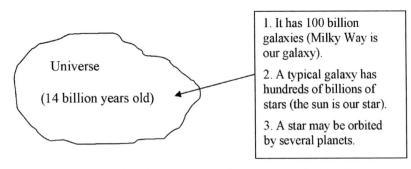

Figure 4.1 Our Universe (not an actual figure)

Some scientists say that there may even be several universes, and physical laws may be different from universe to universe. According to a 2008 study published by a team of scientists led by Alexander Kashlinsky, unseen "structures" are tugging on our universe like cosmic magnets. According to Kashlinsky, an astrophysicist at NASA's Goddard Space Flight Center in Maryland, "Everything in the known universe is said to be racing toward the massive clumps of matter at more than 2 million miles (3.2 million kilometers) an hour—a movement the researchers have dubbed dark flow. The presence of the extra-universal matter suggests that our universe is part of something bigger—a multiverse [multi-universe] —and that whatever is out there is very different from the universe we know." In an attempt to simplify this mind-bending concept, Kashlinsky advises to picture yourself floating in the middle of a vast ocean. As far as the eye can see, the ocean is smooth and identical in every direction, just as most astronomers believe the universe is. You would think, therefore, that beyond the horizon, nothing is different.[5]

"But then you discover a faint but coherent flow in your ocean," Kashlinsky writes. "You would deduce that the entire cosmos is not exactly like what you can see within your own horizon." There must be an out-of-sight mountain river or ravine pushing or pulling the water. Or in the cosmological case, Kashlinsky speculates that "This motion is caused by structures well beyond the current cosmological horizon, which is more than 14 billion light-years away." This theory could rewrite the laws of physics. [6]

If you and your friend are driving vehicles in adjacent lanes on a highway at the same speed along the same direction, you will not mark any movement between yourselves. You can even talk to each other face to face. According to Alexander Kashlinsky's research, the same thing is happening to our entire universe. Our universe is being tugged at two million miles an hour by some unknown forces, as shown in Figure 4.2.

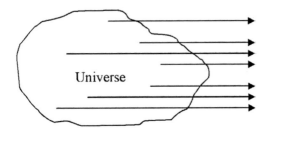

Everything in our universe is being tugged by an unknown force at a speed of 2 million miles an hour.

Figure 4.2 Tugging of Our Universe at 2 Million Miles an Hour (NASA Study)

According to a theory proposed by Neil Turok and Paul Steinhardt, the universe is at least 986 billion years older than physicists had thought. Neil Turok is a theoretical physicist at the University of Cambridge, England, and Paul J. Steinhardt is the Albert Einstein Professor of Science at Princeton University and a professor of theoretical physics. According to them, "The universe must be at least a trillion years old with many big bangs happening before our own. It is a cyclic event that consists of repeating big bangs. With each bang, the theory predicts that matter keeps on expanding and dissipating into infinite space before another horrendous blast of radiation and matter replenishes it. The age of universe is much more likely to be far older than a trillion years though. There doesn't have to be a beginning of time. According to our theory, the universe may be infinitely old and infinitely large."[7]

Distance in astronomy is calculated in terms of light-years. One light-year is equal to the distance traveled by light in one year.

Speed of light = 300,000 kilometers per second

One Light-Year = Distance traveled by light in one year
= 9,460,730,472,580 kilometers

	Approximate Size	Approximate Age
City	10–50 miles	—
Country	100–2,000 miles	—
Earth	3,960 mile radius	4–5 billion years
Our Solar System	Neptune (last planet) is 4 light-years from the sun	4–5 billion years
Milky Way (our galaxy)	Diameter—100,000 light-years Number of stars—200 to 400 billion	13.2 billion years
Universe	Diameter—93 billion light-years	14 billion years
Multiple Big Bangs	—	More than 1 trillion years

Table 4.1 Size and Age of Geographical and Celestial Objects

For example, the sun is at eight light minutes from our earth; that is, light takes about eight minutes to travel ninety-three million miles from the sun to Earth. Hence, if we watch the sun at this moment, we are watching events that took place there eight minutes ago. If, by using the Hubble, we can view galaxies billions of light-years from Earth, we would be witnessing events of billions of years ago. If there are humanlike creatures on a planet that is sixty-five million light-years from Earth, they would be able to see dinosaurs that existed here then. If there are humanlike creatures on a planet twenty-seven hundred light-years from Earth, they would have to wait for another fifty years, seven hundred years, and thirteen hundred years to see the light from Earth during the time of Gautam Buddha (founder of Buddhism), Jesus Christ, and Prophet Muhammad, respectively.

A scientific theory is considered valid only if it is reproducible, that is, it has the following three characteristics:

1. Universal—the theory is applicable to all.
2. Time independent—the theory should be valid today, millions of years ago, and millions of years in the future.
3. Space independent—the theory should be valid everywhere.

For instance, Einstein's famous mass-energy equation, $E = mc^2$, is a scientific law because we will get the same results if we are doing experiments at two different places to verify this law, and this law is not time dependent: it is valid, say, even after ten thousand years.

Suppose I have come up with a scientific theory claiming some kind of output on the basis of some assumptions. Everyone should get the same result at any place and any time if they follow the same assumptions. If anyone gets a different result under the conditions assumed, my theory is invalid.

The big bang theory does not qualify as a scientific principle as it is not reproducible. A theory that explains a one-time phenomenon is not credible, as there would be no way to test it.

Religions and Spirituality

Science discovers the laws of the universe; it does not invent them, as these scientific laws have been used in the universe since time immemorial. Laws we don't yet know may number in the millions. Currently, science has detected and is studying the laws of only about 4 percent of the universe's total energy density. To do this, they use electromagnetic waves, which is the only source of detection available. Scientists are unable to detect the remaining 96 percent (about 22 percent of the mass they call "dark matter"; the remaining 74 percent are "dark energy") [8], as it cannot be detected by electromagnetic waves.

The concept of dark matter is more than seventy-five years old. In 1933, while observing the celestial motions of galaxies in a cluster through his telescope, Fritz Zwicky, of the California Institute of Technology found there should be about several hundred times more estimated mass than was visually observable. Then he came up with this idea of the "missing mass" problem or "dark matter." [9]

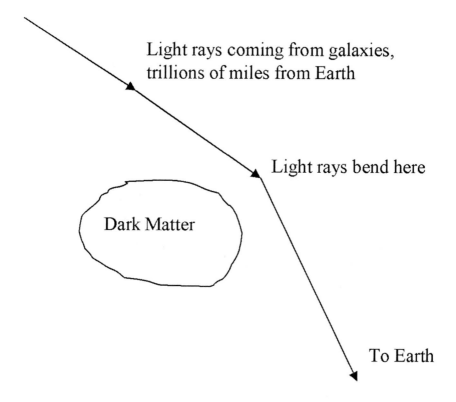

Figure 4.3 Bending of light rays coming from galaxies trillions of miles from Earth, due to dark matter, which cannot be detected by our present-day scientific instruments. Light consists of photons that behave like particles attracted by other objects, in the same way as Earth is attracted by the sun.

Dark matter is detected by its gravitational effects. Recently, a team of seventy astronomers from Europe, America, and Japan used the Hubble space telescope to establish an image of dark matter in a vast region of space where some of the galaxies date back to half the age of the universe: nearly seven billion years. They used a phenomenon known as gravitational lensing, first predicted by Albert Einstein, to investigate an area of the sky nine times the size of a full moon. Gravitational lensing occurs when light from distant galaxies is bent by the gravitational influence of any matter it passes on its journey through space (as shown in figure 4.3). Light consists of photons that behave like particles and is attracted by these galaxies. The scientists were able to exploit the technique by collecting the distorted light from half a million faraway galaxies and reconstructing some of the missing mass of the universe, which is otherwise invisible to the naked eye and conventional telescopes. "We have, for the first time, mapped the large-scale distribution of dark matter in the universe," said Richard Massey of the California Institute of Technology in Pasadena, one of the lead scientists in the team. "Dark matter is a mysterious and invisible form of matter, about which we know very little, yet it dominates the mass of the universe." One of the most important discoveries to emerge from the study is that dark matter appears to form an invisible scaffold or skeleton, around which the visible universe has formed.[10]

According to scientists, some of this dark matter is made up of weakly interacting massive particles (WIMPs) that carry no charge. Scientists say that WIMPs are about one hundred times heavier than protons but rarely interact with ordinary matter. In fact, several billions of WIMPs pass through a human body per second. For more than two decades, scientists have been working hard to learn more about particles like these at deep underground centers like the Cryogenic Dark Matter Search in Soudan, Minnesota; the Boulby Underground Laboratory in Britain; and caverns in Canada, France, Italy, Japan, and Russia.

Scientists are going to great lengths to study the particles that constitute our universe. Neutrinos are subatomic particles that travel at nearly the speed of light, but are so small they can pass undetected through materials without colliding with any molecules. Neutrinos are created as a result of nuclear decay and during nuclear reactions. Trillions of neutrinos pass through our planet without leaving any trace. In order to study neutrinos, US scientists have created a network of 5,160 optical sensors, each about the size of a basketball and suspended on cables in 86 holes, forever embedded in a one kilometer at a South Pole location.

It took almost a decade to build the IceCube Neutrino Observatory. The project was set up at the South Pole because Antarctic polar ice is considered to be pure, transparent, and free of radioactivity. Scientists hope to study blue light emitted by occasional neutrino collision with an atom in ice. In order to detect and study gravitational waves, which are created by black holes, neutron stars, and the big bang—scientists plan to build a telescope, named the Einstein telescope, inside a network of tunnels twelve miles long and a mile underground.

Several other particles like WIMPs and forms of material like dark matter may pervade our universe. But due to its young age, present-day science has no knowledge about them either. From a scientific point of view, our knowledge of the universe is still relatively little. We do, however, know the universe is ancient and our knowledge about it is constantly changing. It benefits us to keep an open mind and not be prejudiced in these matters. Galileo Galilei, who revolutionized astronomy in the seventeenth century, was persecuted, when he claimed Earth revolves around the sun, because it was contradictory to the doctrines of the Church. If Galileo had been allowed to work freely and had received sufficient resources, important scientific work might have been speeded up instead of being silenced.

Limited scientific knowledge has caused us to mystify most physical phenomena and to attribute them to heavenly entities. In some civilizations, earthquakes were explained as being caused by the rumblings of the large snake that held Earth on its head. And those performing so-called miracles (acts generally unknown or unfamiliar) gained popularity and admiration. Fakes, who defrauded people by performing tricks, also gained some influence. In general, however, people followed the paths of those truly endowed with spiritual powers: Krishna, Jesus, Buddha, Moses, and Prophet Muhammad.

While recent advances in scientific and technological knowledge have led to an increase in worldly comforts, we have also witnessed increased skepticism among the scientific community about what we commonly call miracles, parapsychology, or extrasensory perception (ESP). If we are unable to explain such phenomena by current scientific laws, we automatically assume they are fraudulent. But in making such assumptions, we disregard the limited nature of our scientific knowledge. In fact, science has discovered only a small fraction of the laws of nature, and our knowledge is always growing. The sun, for example, has generated energy through nuclear fission for billions of years, but our scientific knowledge of fission was developed only relatively recently by Albert Einstein. About four hundred years ago, Galileo was able to see the moon's craters and Jupiter's satellites through the telescope he developed. But his telescope was primitive compared to the Hubble telescope, which is able to see the birth of new galaxies billions of light-years from Earth. The Hubble telescope will, in turn, prove primitive compared to future telescopes. In fact, once completed in 2012, the planet's largest and most advanced radio telescope, at sixteen thousand feet in the Chilean Andes, will have resolution ten times that of the Hubble. This new telescope will consist of sixty-six radio antennas spread across ten miles. Similarly, more information can be stored on computer hard disks than ever before. The speed of science is ever-accelerating it seems.

Scientific wonders we see today were inconceivable only a few decades ago. Future scientific achievements will advance even further in speed and accuracy. How many and what kind of discoveries await us in the near future is simply unknown to us at present. Today's "miracles" may be explained by some new science in the future.

As our scientific knowledge was severely limited until a couple of hundred years ago, there was some relevancy to the religions that saw light during recent millenniums. From the point of view of religion and spirituality, therefore, we need a theory that is progressive and consistent with the age of the universe and not limited by historical or geographical circumstances. It stands to reason that if there is a God, he would love each and everyone the same—not just those born recently—and he would give everyone—people living here two hundred thousand years ago or humanlike creatures on millions and billions of planets—an equal opportunity to go to heaven or hell or move in any other way. Like any good theory, spiritual theory needs to be free from the distorting influences of time and place.

5

. ◆ .

BRAIN AND SCIENCE

The brain is the center of the nervous system in all vertebrates and most invertebrate, including humans. For an example, humpback whales, great apes (like chimps and orangutans), and dolphins have humanlike brain cells, and they can think.[11] Like humans, chimps and orangutans plan for the future.[12] Birds can distinguish our languages.[13] The human brain, weighing on average about three pounds, is an extremely complex structure that has evolved over millions of years. The difference between a human brain and the brains of other creatures is that the human brain has several capabilities others do not have. Ours is the most advanced brain of all. According to David Linden, a professor of neuroscience at Johns Hopkins University, "Just as the mouse brain is a lizard brain with some extra stuff thrown on top, the human brain is essentially a mouse brain with extra toppings."[14] This is one of the proofs that establishes Darwin's theory of evolution: humans have evolved from animals.

Scientists have observed brain-like functions in plants also. Tiny strangleweed, a pale parasitic plant, can sense the presence of friends, foes, and food and make adroit decisions on how to approach them.[15] Unlike human beings, who may take aspirin as a fever suppressant, stressed plants produce an aspirin-like chemical that can be detected in the air above the plants. This chemical may be a kind of immune response that helps protect the plants. Studies have also shown plants being eaten by animals also produce chemicals that can be sensed by other plants nearby. In addition to having an immune like function, the chemical may be a means for plants to communicate to neighboring plants, warning them of the threat.[16]

The human brain is an extremely complex structure. In a typical human brain, the cerebral cortex (the largest part of brain) is estimated to contain 15–33 billion cells, called neurons,[17] each connected by synapses to several thousand other neurons. A synapse is a structure that permits a neuron to pass an electrical or chemical signal to another cell. Hence synapses are specialized junctions through which neurons signal to each other and to non-neuronal cells. They allow neurons to form circuits within the central nervous system. They allow the nervous system to connect to and control other systems of the body. In layman terms, a neuron has up to ten thousand wires coming out of it and, hence, can connect to up to ten thousand other neurons or non-neuron cells. The adult human brain is estimated to contain from 10^{14} to 5×10^{14} (100–500 trillion) synapses.[18]

A research team from the Humboldt University in Germany and the Erasmus Medical Center in the Netherlands found the simulation of just one rat neuron could deliver the sensation of touch. They stimulated single neurons in rats and found this was enough to trigger a behavioral response when the rats' whiskers were touched. Other US research suggests the computational ability of the brain cell could be even more complex, with different synapses able to act independently from those found elsewhere on the same cell. This could mean that, within a single neuron, different synapses could be storing or processing completely different bits of information, similar to storing files on a computer's hard drive.[19] Therefore, it is beyond present imagination what our brain, with 15-33 billion neurons, each with up to ten thousand synapses, can do if harnessed efficiently.

All five sensory organs (eyes, skin, ears, mouth, and nose) are constantly sending a huge amount of information to the human brain. For example, the eye is forwarding 72 GB (gigabyte, which is equal to one billion bytes) of data each second to the brain. Like radio and television, which tune to a particular frequency, the human brain zeroes in on single bit of information out of the huge amount of data sent to it. Hence, the human brain is very efficient.

We use only a fraction of the capability of our brain. Albert Einstein, whose name is synonymous with genius, died in 1955 at the age of seventy-six. His brain is considered unique[20] and is still preserved. In 1905, he produced five papers that revolutionized how we see the universe. There are other people with unexplored mental potential about whom we have little knowledge. For example, Shakuntala Devi, an Indian whose mind works faster than a computer, calculates multiplication problems and square roots of numbers faster than a supercomputer.

Since brain cells of animals like rats and monkeys are similar to those of humans, neuroscientists are conducting experiments on these animals to develop new medicines and surgeries to treat human behaviors and diseases related to the brain. Scientists have found brain cells that are linked to choice, such as whether to invest in stocks or bonds, and how a person selects different items or goods. They have found neurons involved in assigning values that aid people in making choices. These neurons are in an area of the brain known as the orbitofrontal cortex. They found these neurons while studying monkeys led to choose between different flavors and quantities of juices. Some neurons in the orbitofrontal cortex in monkeys under study were very highly active when they selected three drops of grape juice or ten drops of apple juice.[21]

In the last couple of decades, our knowledge about function and structure of the human brain and their effects on human behavior has improved a lot due to the technologies such as electroencephalography (EEG), magnetoencephalography (MEG), and functional magnetic resonance imaging (fMRI). However, neurologists have just started to scratch the surface. They have a long way to go, as the spatial resolutions of these techniques are very poor.

A day may come when science will be able to analyze the human brain with the help of the computer, which may or may not yield correct results. A computer is defined on the basis of the speed of its processor (megahertz, gigahertz, etc.), hard drive size (in gigabyte), and memory size (in gigabyte). A hertz is one CPU (Central Processing Unit) cycle. These cycles are the frequency within which CPUs execute instructions. A computer with one gigahertz processor executes instructions one billion times per second, but the type of chip used in the processor also matters.

Today's computers may or may not present the correct model of the human brain. Each human brain is unique in construction, that is, the locations of hard drive and memory may not be at the same places in every human being. Apart from this, it is proven clinically that the human brain generates new cells at any age.[22]

One discovery surprised the neurosurgeons at the Toronto Western Hospital, Ontario. They were operating on a brain of a 419 pound (190 kg) obese man to control his appetite. They inserted electrodes on the hypothalamus, which controls appetite, and stimulated it with an electric current. Instead of suppressing the appetite, it improved his memory. He recalled, in intricate detail, a scene from thirty years earlier. According to neurosurgeons, "He reported the experience of being in a park with friends from when he was around 20 years old and, as the intensity of stimulation increased, the details became more vivid. He recognized his girlfriend [at the time] … The scene was in color. People were wearing identifiable clothes and were talking, but he could not decipher what they were saying." The hypothalamus was not usually identified as a seat of memory. The contacts that most readily produced memories were located close to a structure called the fornix, an arched bundle of fibers that carries signals within the limbic system, which is situated next to the hypothalamus. [23]

According to Professor Andres Lozano, "His performance improved dramatically. As we turned the current up, we first drove his memory circuits and improved his learning. As we increased the intensity of the current, we got spontaneous memories of discrete events. At a certain intensity, he would slash to the scene [in the park]. When the intensity was increased further, he got more detail, but when the current was turned off, it rapidly decayed. This is the first time that anyone has had electrodes implanted in the brain which have been shown to improve memory. We are driving the activity of the brain by increasing its sensitivity—turning up the volume of the memory circuits. Any event that involves the memory circuits is more likely to be stored and retained." Professor Lozano is a neurosurgeon at the Toronto Western Hospital, Ontario, and a world authority on deep-brain stimulation. He has performed four hundred operations on individuals with Parkinson's disease. [24]

This shows there is a lot on our brain's hard drive (brain cells where we store our memories), but we cannot get to some of these portions of our hard drive: we cannot read from these brain cells.

Here, I would like to discuss another observation. During emergencies, time seems to slow down. Sometimes minutes seem to last for hours. According to research conducted at Baylor College of Medicine, this is due to a trick played by one's memory. When a person is scared, a brain area called the amygdala becomes more active, laying down an extra set of memories that go along with those normally taken care of by other parts of brain. David Eagleman, a neuroscientist at Baylor College of Medicine said, "In this way, frightening events are associated with richer and denser memories and the more memory you have an event, the longer you believe it took." This also explains why we as a child lay down rich memories of all our experiences, but when we are older, we lay down fewer memories. Therefore, when a child looks back at the end of a summer, it seems to have lasted forever; adults think it zoomed by.[25]

Some Recent Advances in Brain Study and Their Practical Uses

1. In 2002, the scientists at Downstate Medical Center, in Brooklyn, New York, were able to remote control rats by placing electrodes inside their brains, effectively turning them into remote-controlled robots, like remote-controlled cars. They placed the electrodes in the somatosensory cortex part of the rats' brain, which receives signals when their whiskers brush against an object. When scientists activated the electrode in the left somatosensory cortex, the rat turned right, as if it thought its right whiskers brushed against an object. (The left brain gets signals from the body's right side and vice versa.) Scientists were able to make the rat turn left, right, or move forward based on which electrode was stimulated.[26]

2. Available on the market are toys that read a user's brain waves or the brain's electrical signals and, in turn, operate remote-controlled objects. You can get these toys for about $80-$90. The basis of these toys is the EEG: the recording of electrical activity through electrodes placed along the scalp, produced by the firing of neurons within the brain.

3. People with severe disabilities who cannot operate a hand-controlled motorized wheelchair can operate one using an electrode-lined skullcap which is first calibrated by storing brain scans for his thoughts, for an example his intention to move left or right. Then for his subsequent actions, his brain is first

scanned by the skullcap which compares it with stored brain scans. Depending on the outcome of the match of the brain scan, the wheelchair moves left, right, straight, goes up, or goes down. Similarly, scientists have implanted electrodes in the motor cortex part, which controls movement of limbs, of the brain of people with severe disabilities to capture movement of neurons in brain, and in turn, the electrodes move the cursor on the computer screen. They were able to open e-mails and websites, and do what a person without disabilities can do on a computer.

4. Using fMRI, a group of scientists, led by John Dylan Haynes of Max Plank Institute for Human Cognitive and Brain Sciences in Germany, was able to predict a person's intentions with 70 percent accuracy. The study revealed signatures of activity in a marble-sized part of the brain called the medial prefrontal cortex that changed when a person intended to add or subtract numbers.[27] Three to four decades ago, we did not have software or enough hardware (computing power/speed of processor, as well as enough memory size and hard drive capacity) for speech recognition. But now, speech recognition software is used everywhere. Instead of pressing buttons on phone, you just speak the numbers or names, and the software recognizes all the alphanumeric characters using pattern recognition software. Similarly, the resolutions of brain scanning techniques are in primitive stage: that is, very low. Once resolution capabilities reach very minute levels, science may be able to scan and read brain cells, predicting even the intentions of human beings. If it becomes successful, it can prevent crimes, as shown in the 2002 film *Minority Report*.

6

• ◆ •

MIND, TANTRA, AND MANTRA

Tantra

Although the evolution of human beings in their present form may be traced back two hundred thousand years, human civilization is only between ten thousand and fifteen thousand years old. In the hoary past, humanlike beings focused on fulfilling their physical needs. Gradually, they started to worship objects found in nature—like rivers, stones, and hills—to quell their primitive fears and superstitiously appease assumed natural divinities.

About ten thousand years ago, saints in Asia began to explore the human mind and its relationship with the infinite. They had found limitations in physical pleasure and intellectual knowledge and wanted to go beyond. These saints found wonderful results. At any time, we may enjoy only a limited amount of physical pleasures. We can eat only a limited amount of good food, and after some time, we will again feel hungry. Even if we amass a lot of money and power, we will find someone with more money or someone more powerful.

A human being is never satisfied with the materialistic world. A Wall Street banker wants million dollar bonuses every year. In the realm of intellectual knowledge, we can always find millions of books we have not read. We can always find people who have much more knowledge in areas where we have limited knowledge.

When Isaac Newton saw an apple falling from a tree, he came up with his famous Laws of Motion. Similarly, when saints in Asia started exploring functions of their minds and how everything around them was created, they came up with a wonderful theory called Tantra. The word "tan" means "to expand," and "tra" means "liberator." Hence, Tantra is the science of liberation from all type of bondages—physical, mental, and spiritual.

Tantric saints wrote texts based on their experiences. They researched their minds and discovered mental exercises, like meditation practices for controlling the mind—a person's most vital organ and the one that feels pain and happiness. These saints also discovered words (mantras) that, when chanted rhythmically, create acoustic waves that produce electrical signals in the brain and physical body for desired effects. Some of these saints composed the Vedas, the oldest sacred books in existence. The origins of the first Veda, *Rigveda*, can be traced back fifteen thousand years. Its composition continued until five thousand years ago. The other three Vedas are *Yajurvada, Atharvaveda,* and *Samaveda* (the latter is a collection of songs and hymns from the three preceding Vedas).

According to Shrii Shrii Anandamurti ji, "About 7,000 years ago, the metamorphosed form of Tantra became *taota*. Taota after further distortion and further metamorphosis, became *taoa*—in modern Chinese language it became *tao* and then *Taoism*. The Sanskrit *dhyána* became *c'han* in Chinese, c'han became *chen* in Korean, chen became *zen* in Japanese."[28]

In many tribal areas today, as well as ancient cultural practices, people use traditional medicines. Some of these naturopathic treatments are very effective. Chinese acupuncture, Indian Ayurveda, and Unani medicines all fall into this category. The developers of these systems did not conduct rigorous research using modern, complex scientific instruments. They did not attempt to determine the chemical compositions of the remedies. Their only interest was the effectiveness of the cure. For example, Indians have known about the medicinal use of neem (Azadirachta) and turmeric (Curcuma) for several thousands of years. Neem is used in Ayurveda as a medicine for skin diseases and other ailments. Neem-based products are antifungal, sedating, antidiabetic, antibacterial, and antiviral. Turmeric is antiseptic and anti-inflammatory. It may also be applied directly to the skin for eczema and to help heal wounds. The US National Institutes of Health has been conducting clinical trials to study the anti-inflammatory effects of turmeric in treatment for certain types of cancers, including multiple myeloma, and Alzheimer's disease.

In chapter 5, we discussed the evolution of the human brain. Now we look at the evolution of the mind in view of the age-old Indian philosophy that predates Hinduism. According to the big bang theory, the Universe was once in an extremely hot and dense state which expanded rapidly and it is still expanding. But the big bang theory fails to explain what existed before that evolution and to where the universe is expanding. The evolution theory, discussed in this chapter, answers both these two questions.

Unique Characteristic of Mind

From a philosophical point of view, the brain is a physical structure controlled by the mind. But there is a fundamental difference between the concept of mind and the brain we discussed in the last chapter or what neurologists consider: that is, a structure consisting of one hundred billion neurons. The brain can multitask, but the mind cannot.

Everything you do is either controlled by your brain or your brain gets information about this activity. If you are moving your hand and leg simultaneously, it is your brain that is doing these two functions; your brain is simultaneously sending signals to both the hand and leg to move. On the other hand, the mind has a unique characteristic. In any given instant, it can focus on only one subject. We see this unique characteristic in daily life. If someone is walking on the road thinking about something, he might ignore his best friend, who happens to be standing on the pavement. At that time, his eyes were working and the friend's picture was being formed on his retina, but as his mind was busy with something else, he was not taking notice of the information sent by the eye. Similarly, if someone is eating and reading an interesting book simultaneously, he might not notice the lack of salt in the food. As his mind is busy with reading, the information sent by his tongue (the food being less salty) to the mind is blocked. This also shows that it is up to the mind to utilize the functions of sensory organs and not the other way around. A sensory organ cannot force the mind to do something. Later in this chapter, we will see the mind is the mechanic and brain is the machine.

Constituents of Mind

Figure 6.1 shows the components of a vehicle, whether it is a bicycle, car, or space shuttle. For a bicycle, the engine denotes the pedals, and the transmission system is the two large wheels, run by the chain connected to the pedals. For a car, the engine denotes a four- or six-cylinder engine, and the transmission denotes the transmission shafts and four wheels.

Figure 6.1 The Components of a Vehicle

Let us now discuss the components of our mind. According to Shrii Shrii Anandamurti ji, our mind consists of three parts: mind stuff (*citta*), doer-"I" (*ahamtattva*), and "I" exist (*mahattattva*). Suppose you are looking at John. Your eyes receive light waves (vibrations) of John. (Information like smell, touch, taste, and light waves comes from outside, strikes our sensory organs, and travels in our body through the firing of nerve cells or neuron movements. We will call these vibrations.) Your eyes project the image of John onto your retina, which fires appropriate nerve cells to carry this information to the brain. Then, the brain conveys this information to the mind. You "see" John in your mind and not in your brain. Hence, there have to be at least two parts of a mind: one that "becomes" John and another that "sees" John. These vibrations are also stored in your brain's nerve cells.

When you close your eyes and think about John, your mind re-creates John's image. When you re-create John, a part of your mind becomes John, and another part of your mind sees him, just like when you saw his physical self. The part of mind that becomes John is the mind stuff (inner circle in figure 6.2), and the part of mind that sees him is called doer-"I" (the part between the inner circle and middle circle in figure 6.2). But in order for these two to exist, there has to be a third part of mind, which gives the feeling of existence of I. This third part of mind, or I, is called "I" exist (the part between middle circle and outer circle in figure 6.2). "Mind" is the collective name of these three elements: mind stuff, doer "I," and "I" exist. The existence of I in the mind only proves that there is another real entity beyond mind that knows of the existence of mind. This supreme witnessing entity is called Atman, or soul, or unit consciousness.

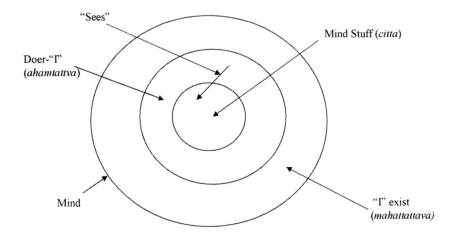

Figure 6.2 Three Parts of Mind

Evolution of Mind

In Tantra, there are two types of consciousness: non-qualified consciousness (*Nirguńa Brahma*) and qualified consciousness (*Saguńa Brahma*). Apart from this, there is the cosmic operative principle, which constitutes three types of fundamental forces that maintain order in the entire universe. In non-qualified consciousness, the three fundamental forces of the cosmic operative principle balance each other, and, hence, there is no expression. Under certain conditions, the non-qualified consciousness converts into qualified consciousness because of the cosmetic operative principle. In the process of cosmic centrifugal activity (*saincara*), five fundamental factors— ethereal, aerial, luminous, liquid, and solid—are made out of qualified consciousness, with solid being the crudest out of the five. These changes happen gradually.

In some conditions, a unit mind is created inside an object in the cosmic centripetal process (*pratisaincara*) due to the attractive force of

Supreme Consciousness. Initially, the unit mind is almost entirely made up of mind stuff; these species are underdeveloped creatures and plants. Gradually, the same unit mind takes the form of higher and higher species—like plants, animals, vertebrates, mammals, and so on—as the other two parts of the mind, the portions of doer-"I" and "I" exist, increase as shown in figure 6.3. The human being is the highest. We know plants and trees also have brain/mind, as they also feel pain.[29] The concept of the evolution of mind is shown in figure 6.3. According to one school of Indian philosophy, there are 8.4 million species in the world.

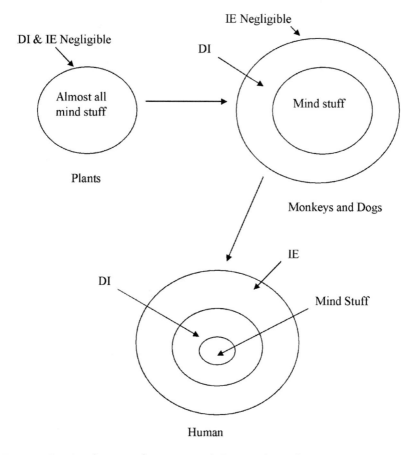

Figure 6.3 Evolution of Unit Mind (DI and IE denote Doer-"I" and "I"-Exist, respectively)

All seeds may not sprout. Some seeds may be bad or lack properties required for sprouting. A good seed will sprout only if it has the proper environment (earth, air, water, light, and so on). Similarly, a unit mind is not created inside all objects in qualified consciousness. Therefore, ideation on crude subjects, like idols, does not lead to non-qualified consciousness.

Species with undeveloped minds are mostly guided by the cosmic operative principle. They evolve routinely, as they are guided by their instincts. These species are not aware of the reactions of their actions, because their consciousnesses are not developed. Except some creatures, like monkeys and dogs, the doer-"I" is not developed. Trained monkeys and dogs may have a little more intelligence than other animals. Domesticated animals can feel the pain and pleasure of their masters.

Suppose a buffalo sees a farm with green grass. It will impulsively go there to eat. You, on the other hand, will first check your wallet before entering a restaurant. If you have no money, you will not enter. This is the difference between an animal and a human. A human is a rational animal. Both a human and an animal have inborn instincts, but a human is guided by intellect. Animals are generally guided by those instincts, unless it is taught otherwise.

As human beings have developed consciousness and know the reaction of their actions, they are liable for those actions. Hence, they may either go forward to become a godly like soul (get salvation and even merge in the non-qualified consciousness) or go backward, toward animals and plants. As the unit mind of a human being has evolved from that of an animal, it has tendency to go after the physical world (eating, drinking, sex, and so on), like animals, unless it gets proper guidance.

Humans have three ways of expression: thinking, speaking, and action. Since an animal does not have a developed mind, it does not have coordination among these three expressions. Therefore, humans, who also do not have coordination among these three expressions, are worse than animals, because humans have a developed mind, which they may use. Right now, this type of human being is in the majority in our society. The second type of humans are those who have coordination in speaking and action: that is, whatever they say, they do. But they have a deficiency, because they do not think along the same line as they speak and act. The most refined type of human beings are those with coordination in thinking, speaking, and action. Whatever they think, they speak and do. Such people can be considered next to God.

As plants and trees are made up of trillions of undeveloped cells/minds with no developed mind (mostly made up of mind stuff), you can cut parts of them and replant in another place, where they will grow into mature plants of their own. On the other hand, animals and human beings have developed minds; their minds reflect mind stuff and varying degrees of the other two (doer-"I" and "I" exist). There is no way to multiply such beings by cutting them into pieces, like plants.

The universe is qualified consciousness (Saguna Brahma) created out of non-qualified consciousness (Nirguna Brahma) because of the forces of the cosmic operative principle. Qualified consciousness is like a finite iceberg in an infinite ocean, and our universe is like an iceberg in an infinite ocean.

There is a saying in Hindi language, *Kan kan mein Bhagwan*: There is God in each and every particle. The theory described above supports this saying.

Sometimes, normally only a few times in the course of one's life, a unit mind's doer-"I" can tap into the Cosmic doer-"I," as it is part of it. At that time, the person will know what another person is thinking or what he is going to do: the Cosmic mind has all that information. This incident is called telepathy.

Sensory and Motor Organs

The mind is the master of our biological machine. It gets information, analyzes it, and acts. It gets information from the outside world via

43

sensory organs and acts via motor organs. Human beings have five sensory and five motor organs. Sensory organs get vibrations from the outside world, and motor organs send vibrations to the outside world.

Sensory organs and their functions are:

1. eye (sight)
2. nose (smell)
3. ear (hearing)
4. tongue (taste)
5. skin (touch)

Motor organs are:

1. vocal cords (speak)
2. legs (movement)
3. hands (work)
4. anus (to expel feces)
5. genital organs (for creating life and giving birth)

Yoga

The majority of people in the West consider yoga as just some physical exercises, but the physical exercises are only one of the eight elements of Raja Yoga. Physical yoga (exercises) is to make the body and mind fit for meditation.

In Tantra, the word "yoga" is derived from the Sanskrit root word *yunj,* which means unification. Yoga is the unification of the human soul (*atman*) with the Cosmic Soul (*Paramatman*), or God, in which the souls no long have a separate identity. When you add two apples to three apples, those five apples do not constitute yoga, as the apples still have separate identities. On the other hand, when a drop of water joins an ocean, it may be considered as yoga, because the drop of water loses its identity after joining the ocean. A second definition of yoga was given by Patanjali. According to him, yoga is the suspension of all mental propensities.

Patanjali's Astanga-Yoga (a system of Raja Yoga), meaning eight-limbed yoga, has the following elements:

1. Yama: nonviolence, nonlying, nonstealing, nonsensuality, and nonpossessiveness
2. Niyama: purity, contentment, austerity, study, and surrender to God
3. Asana: yogic exercises
4. Pranayama: breath control
5. Pratyahara: withdrawal of the sensory organs from external objects
6. Dharana: concentration or fixing the mind on a single object
7. Dhyana: intense contemplation of the nature of the object of meditation
8. Samādhi: oneness with God

Chakras and Propensities

Although the first written mention of chakras (here, "chakra" means a psychospiritual plexus) can be found in the Upanishads written around 1200–900 BC. Chakras were known in South Asia for several thousand years before the Upanishads were written. When the Vedas were composed, there was no script, and people did not know how to write. Hence, they passed on their knowledge orally. For this very reason, the Vedas are termed as *sruti,* meaning memorized texts.

According to the Upanishads, there are seven main chakras in a human body. In the last century, our science found these chakras actually manifest as glands. The seven main chakras are:

1. muladhara chakra: midpoint of the last vertebra of the spinal column
2. svadhisthana chakra: situated at the back of the genital organs
3. manipura chakra: at the navel
4. anahata chakra: at the center of chest
5. vishuddha chakra: at the top of the spine and associated with thyroid gland
6. ajina chakra: between the eyebrows and associated with pituitary gland
7. sahasrara chakra: the crown of the head and associated with pineal gland

The secretion of hormones from these glands affects our body. Any under- or over-secretion of hormones has physical and psychological effects. The secretion from an upper gland affects the lower ones, but not vice versa. The secretion from the pineal gland (which is the uppermost gland) affects all other glands in the body.

The operative center of the mind stuff and the mind exits in the sixth chakra, the ajina chakra, situated at the pineal gland or between the two eyebrows. From ajina chakra, the mind indirectly controls the sensory organs.

According to Shrii Shrii Anandamurti ji, "Besides the main nerve centers at the point of each chakra, there are also sub-centers where sub-glands are located. These sub-glands influence [and control] the propensities attached to each chakra. This science is largely unknown today."[30]

In the manipura chakra, there is the maximum accumulation of heat. It is the shelter of heat, and is known as *agnyashaya* in Sanskrit. It is also known as *mahashaya*, meaning "the shelter of greatness", because it is the centre of the body. According to Shrii Shrii Anandamurti ji, there are ten glands and sub-glands around this chakra. When a person dies and is cremated, often the navel does not get fully burnt, which is why it is a common practice in India for people to throw the remains of a dead body into a river. The burning point of the navel is higher than the temperature generated by an ordinary funeral pyre. The navel will only be completely destroyed if the body is allowed to burn for a long time and is cremated with enormous heat.

The anahata chakra is connected with the respiratory system. According to Shrii Shrii Anandamurti ji, there are twelve sub-glands near this chakra. *Naksattras* influence the area around this chakra in the human body, rather of all bodies. Naksa means "to twinkle." Naksattras are stars several light years from our solar system. The original light from stars, the reflected and refracted light from planets, satellites and meteors, and the light from galaxies and nebulae reflect on all the glands and sub-glands of the body, and especially on the anahata chakra. The reflecting plate of the anahata chakra is a bit bigger than the anahata chakra itself.

There are fifty main propensities of mind. They function internally and externally. For example, one can steal both mentally and physically. Hence, every propensity can function in two ways. Apart from this, there are ten sensory and motor organs. Therefore, a human mind has a total of one thousand expressions (50 × 2 × 10), or mental occupations. The controlling point of these one thousand expressions is the sahasrara chakra (pineal gland). In Sanskrit, *sahasrara* means one thousand. According to Shrii Shrii Anandamurti, the propensities associated with each chakra are:[31]

Muladhara chakra

1. psycho-spiritual longing
2. psychic longing

3. physical longing
4. spiritual longing

Svadhisthana chakra

1. indifference
2. lack of common sense
3. indulgence
4. lack of confidence
5. thought of sure annihilation
6. cruelty

Manipura chakra

1. shyness
2. sadistic tendency
3. envy
4. staticity, sleepiness
5. melancholia
6. peevishness
7. yearning for acquisition
8. infatuation
9. hatred, revulsion
10. fear

Anahata chakra

1. hope
2. worry
3. endeavor
4. mine-ness, love
5. vanity

6. conscience, discrimination
7. mental numbness due to fear
8. ego
9. avarice
10. hypocrisy
11. argumentativeness to point of wild exaggeration
12. repentance

Vishuddha chakra

1. sound of peacock
2. sound of ox
3. sound of goat
4. sound of deer
5. sound of cuckoo
6. sound of donkey
7. sound of elephant
8. acoustic root of creation, preservation, dissolution
9. sound of arousing kulakundalinii
10. practication, i.e., putting a theory into practice
11. expression of mundane knowledge
12. welfare in the subtler sphere
13. performing noble actions
14. surrender to the Supreme
15. repulsive expression
16. sweet expression

Ajina chakra

1. mundane knowledge
2. spiritual knowledge

All the propensities except spiritual knowledge are related to mind's ties to matter. Only the last propensity is the mind's connection with the spirit. About two thousand years ago, Astavakra, a great saint, wrote a book, *Aśtávakra Saṁhitá,* in which he discussed the process of controlling all the chakras and their propensities.

Hence a chakra is a collection of glands and sub-glands, and the location of these glands and sub-glands differs from animal to animal. In humans the chakras are situated at the intersecting points of the ida, susumna and piungala, three psycho-spiritual channels. Each of these three psycho-spiritual channels starts from the muladhar chakra, runs nearly parallel to the spinal cord and ends at the sahasrara chakra. In the human mind various thoughts are constantly emerging and dissolving. Behind these psychic phenomena are the underlying vrttis (propensities) which are primarily related to the inborn samskaras also called karma or mental reactive momenta (as explained in next chapter) of a human being. Propensities are formed according to one's inherent samskaras, and the expression and control of these propensities are dependent upon the various chakras. The fifty main propensities of the human mind are expressed internally or externally through the vibrational expression of these chakras. These vibrations cause hormones to be secreted from the glands, and the natural or unnatural expression of the propensities depends on the degree of normal or abnormal secretion of the hormones.

It is a tradition in India that a saint blesses a disciple by placing his hand on the disciple's head. Actually, the saint is placing the hand on the sahasrára chakra of the disciple, which has a positive effect on all the other chakras.

During yogic exercises, subtle pressure of asana on a gland restores the balance of hormonal secretion. These exercises have a pressurizing or depressurizing effect on the glands. For example, the mayurasana (peacock posture) has a pressurizing effect on the manipura chakra. A person with a great fear of public speaking usually has a weak manipura chakra. He or she should regularly do the peacock posture to cure their fear of public speaking.

Extreme fear causes excessive tension and pressure on the manipura chakra. Usually, when people experience fear, the afferent and efferent nerves are able to work properly. The tension in the nerves caused by the fear travels through the nervous system and reaches the brain, so excessive pressure does not occur. However, when a person becomes extremely fearful, the balance between the afferent and efferent nerves is lost, and there is a buildup of tension and pressure around the manipura chakra. If the information carried by the efferent nerves from the brain to the manipura chakra is prevented from reaching its destination, the imbalance can cause a blockage in the region of the anáhata chakra, which is a very complicated and sensitive part of the human body. A disturbance in this region can cause palpitations, excessive pressure on the heart, the inability to act decisively, and even a heart attack. [32]

The human body is a biological machine, and every part has an important function. Humans have joint hair near the lymphatic glands in the armpits and leg joints. Joint hair works as a heat dissipater similar to a radiator in an automobile. If this hair is removed, it causes overheating of the lymphatic glands and oversecretion of hormones, which also decreases the function of the thyroid gland.

In Tantra, there is the concept of *kundalini*, also called the coiled serpentine. "Coiled" implies that potential energy is in coiled form. Kundalini resides at the lowest chakra, at the muladhara. When a person does meditation, the kundalinii rises from the lowest chakra and moves to upper chakras, one after another. At different chakras, it takes control of all the propensities associated with the respective chakras. Once it reaches the topmost sahasrara chakra, the aspirant feels oneness with Supreme Consciousness (a state of Nirvikalpa Samadhi).

Memory: How It Works

Memory is the re-creation of things already perceived. Once the mind stuff has perceived an object, a certain vibration corresponding to the perceived object is stored in the nerve cells; mind stuff contains the seed of the corresponding experience. Re-creating the same feeling in the mind stuff by retrieving the vibrations from the nerve cells is called memory. Therefore, the base of memory is not in the brain but in the mind stuff.

Through one's sensory organs, a human being receives five kinds of vibrations from an object. These vibrations are sound, touch, shape, taste, and smell. Although the sensory organs receive the vibrations from the outside objects, it is the brain, in conjunction with the mind, that feels it. For example, when someone speaks, the sound vibration strikes the ear canal, which in turn, fires nerve cells the send this information to the brain and then finally to the mind. The sound vibrations generated outside are distinct in nature; otherwise, you will not able to differentiate who has spoken. Similarly, the smell of a flower emanates smell vibrations that strike our nose, which in turn, fires appropriate nerve cells, sending this information to the brain and mind. These incidents are stored in brain nerve cells as distinct vibrations. It is the doer-"I" who re-creates these incidents in the mind stuff, with the help of these vibrations. In a recorded CD-ROM or DVD-ROM, you cannot see the songs or movie with your eyes. You require certain devices to hear the songs or watch the movies recorded on them. Similarly, it is the doer-"I" that has the key to play the re-created the memory stored in a human mind's nerve cells, and the seed is in the mind stuff.

When you see Niagara Falls for the first time, its vibrations will be stored in your brain cells, and the mind stuff alone has its seed. In the future, when you would like to "see" the Niagara Falls again, your doer-"I" will request your mind stuff to activate the appropriate vibrations stored in the brain nerve cells and then make the image of Niagara Falls in the mind stuff. On its own, the mind stuff cannot perform any function. It acts on the will of doer-"I." If the doer-"I" wants the mind stuff to see something, the mind stuff will bring the visual vibrations from the eyes/retina or stored visual vibrations from brain nerve cells and become the image. If doer-"I" wants to hear something, the mind stuff will bring stored sound vibrations from the ear and hearing-related brain cells and become sound.

Let us discuss dreams. When awake and thinking about your sister, her image appears in your mind. Because you are conscious, you know whatever you are seeing is not real. On the other hand, if you see something in your mind during dreams, it seems real to you, as your conscious mind is not working at that time. Therefore, during dreams, you may do something (like speak something, kick your legs, spread your hands, and so on) you would not have done in a similar situation while awake.

Nothing in this world is static. Everything in this universe has a vibrational nature. Shrii Shrii Anandamurti ji quoted Nobel laureate Rabindranath Tagore: "'When I sketch any object, when any object is drawn, it does not lose its mobility.'" When you see a picture, you cannot deny it has mobility. If you say something is confined within the scope of lines, is presented as a picture, and, as such, is static, you are wrong. Because the idea represented by the picture enters your mind and vibrates it, and you cannot confine those vibrations, you cannot declare anything to be static or inert.

Kii pralάp kahe kavi,
Nahe nahe nahe shudhu chabi;
Ke bale, rayeche sthira;
Mari mari sei saondaryya
Nibhe yeta yadi

"What a meaningless utterance the poet has made! No, no, no, it is not simply a picture! Who says it is static? It would be a great tragedy if that beauty vanished."[33]

Mantra

According to a study on Tibetan Buddhist monks in India conducted by researchers at the University of Queensland and the University of California, Berkeley, the monks were able to focus on just one image, whereas, most people's attention would fluctuate. According to the monks, this is why they are able not to dwell on negative things that happen. They digest it and just move on.[34]

Using brain scanning techniques, neuroscientists at the University of Wisconsin at Madison showed activity in the left prefrontal lobes of experienced Buddhist practitioners. This happens even when they are not meditating. This area is linked to positive emotions, self-control, and temperament. According to Paul Ekman, of the University of California San Francisco Medical Center, meditation and mindfulness can tame the amygdala, an area of the brain that is the hub of fear memory. He discovered that experienced Buddhists were less likely to be shocked, flustered, surprised, or as angry as other people.[35]

It has been scientifically proven that if a person's mind is disturbed, the electrical waves generated by his or her mind are irregular. But if a person is cool and calm, the waves are regular and systematic. The electrical measurements of brain activity produce four types of waves: alpha, beta, theta, and delta. During meditation, the brain produces mostly alpha waves, which denote restful alertness.

When a person is angry, his face becomes red, and his limbs start to tremble; he cannot speak properly. All these happen within fractions of second because of the violent vibration in his brain. Thereafter, he cannot think properly about what is wrong or right. He loses his appetite. This shows that each and every cell of a human body is controlled by the brain and, in turn, by mind.

Mantras have emerged in the Sanskrit language, because the combinations of acoustic sounds generated by the Sanskrit alphabets have particularly profound effects on the body's chakras and mind. When you expand your mind through proper meditation, your mind expands, ripping apart the forces of the cosmic operative principle in the same way you could break a chain by expanding your body if your body were chained.

As explained in figure 6.4, meditation and systematic chanting of mantras superimpose regularity and system on the irregular mental waves a person may be experiencing. Prolonged chanting of mantras and meditation enable a person to make his or her mental waves regular and systematic. When you think something, you are speaking mentally; that is, you are creating neuron movements.

Figure 6.4 Types of Waves

(a) Regular Wave

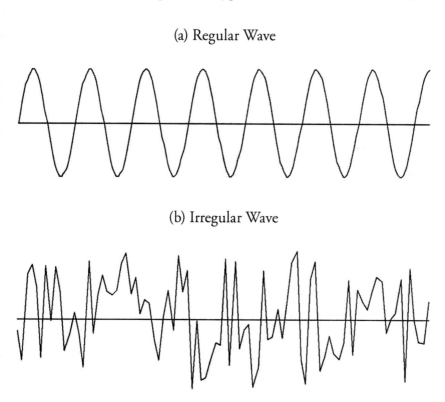

(b) Irregular Wave

The purpose of meditation is to control the mind and then to control the sensory organs and the propensities of mind. Therefore, the practice of mantra recitation helps to establish parallelism between a person's external physical vibration and his internal vibration. When we place our mind at one chakra and recite the appropriate mantra, it creates neuron movement that, in turn, helps purify the chakra/gland and its associated propensities.

While doing meditation, a person may achieve his final goal: the achievement of Nirvikalpa Samadhi (to feel oneness with the Supreme Consciousness) by getting his or her kundalini to the topmost chakra (Sahasrara Chakra). But he or she may not experience any significant spiritual experiences during the entire process. For example, while flying from Los Angeles to New York, you may not realize you are passing cities like Albuquerque, St Louis, Chicago, Cleveland, and Philadelphia.

There are two types of meditation practitioners in Tantra. *Vidya sadhana* (spiritual meditation) is done for self-realization, whereas, *avidya sadhana* (profane meditation) is done to control the material world. In the long run, avidya sadhana leads to self-destruction.

Significance of Aum

Aum (also known as om, pranava, omkara, and onmkara) is a mystical or sacred syllable in the Indian religions, including Hinduism, Sikhism, Jainism, and Buddhism.

Figure 6.5 Aum

Every action creates a sound. People, machines (like automobiles and planes, and so on), the environment, and so on generate a huge sound in, say, Los Angeles. When Earth moves around the sun, it creates a sound, although we cannot hear it. Scientists working at the Large Hadron Collider, where they are generating subatomic particles, have found that subatomic particles also generate sounds.

When you go to a crowded mall, you hear several dozens of people speaking simultaneously. You will hear people saying, for example, "This shoe looks very nice," "This shirt is very costly," "This jacket will not fit me," … When you come out of the mall, you will not hear these individual sentences. Instead, you will hear something like, "Hamannnamanalkaala." That is, you will not be able to distinguish anything specific or understand what it means.

If you are driving a car on the highway, you hear the sound generated by your car and a few other vehicles around your car. On the other hand, if you live near an interstate highway, you will hear the indistinct sum of all kinds of sounds coming from the direction of interstate highway. This sum-sound is a combination of the sounds generated by hundreds of vehicles on the highway.

Humans can hear sounds with frequencies between 20 Hz and 20 kHz (called the audio range). The human ear cannot catch sound vibrations below or above this range. Light waves with a wavelength between 400 nm and 700 nm are visible to us, and we cannot see any light waves above or below this range. Animals like bats and owls can see in the dark, but we cannot.

At any given time, there are trillions of waves traveling around us, but we are not aware of them. Among their sources are cell phones, radio stations, TV stations, wireless transmissions, and people speaking to each other. The function of a TV is to filter one particular wave out of these trillions of waves and display it on the screen. Similarly, the function of a cell phone is to filter a particular wave (corresponding to the phone number associated with the particular phone) out of trillions of waves.

The science of Tantra has developed over ten thousand years. Scores of saints in Asia have researched their minds and the effects of Sanskrit mantras on their minds. Most of their results are beyond the scope of present-day science. With the help of proper meditation and mantras, one can listen to transcendent sounds or see waves beyond the normal.

When you think something, you are speaking mentally; that is, you are creating neuron movements. Suppose while at work, you think, *During the long weekend, I will go to Florida.* You are speaking this sentence mentally, and others cannot hear. The neuron movements in your brain create vibrations others cannot capture. With the help of meditation, one can hear the sound generated in the mind and the divine sound.

Aum is of great significance in Tantra. Aum consists of three letters: a, u, and ma. A is the sound of creation, u is the sound of retention, and ma is the sound of destruction. Auma, or aum, is the collective sound of all the works being done in the universe. When someone elevates the kundalini to ajina chakra (pituitary gland), he or she will come in contact with non-qualified consciousness (Saguna Brahma) and can hear the sound aum.[36]

Under a tree in Bodh Gaya, India, Gautama Buddha, the founder of Buddhism, attained enlightenment when he was able to raise his kundalini to the topmost chakra and tune in to the Cosmic Mind.

Be the Master of Organs

Despite their best efforts, students are often unable to concentrate on the teacher's lecture. The subjects on their mind change from time to time. If at one moment a student's mind is focused on the lecture, within some seconds, its attention may change to a movie, then to his or her residence, and so on. This shows the student is not a master of his or her mind. Instead, the mind is that student's master.

One characteristic of the sensory organs is they go after external objects. The eyes constantly send light vibrations to the retina, and from there, nerve cells send vibrations to the mind. The ears send every sound vibration from the surrounding objects to the mind. The other three sensory organs are doing the same. It is up to the mind to select one out of these or to re-create a vibration from memory in the mind stuff. Depending on its karma (to be described in the next chapter) and the environment, the mind either selects the vibrations on its own or is influenced by vibrations received from the sensory organs. The organs should be controlled by the mind and not the other way around.

If you eat some good food, it feels good on the tongue before it enters the digestive system. From the tongue, the taste feeling (vibration) is relayed through the nerve cells to the mind stuff, where the doer-"I" captures the taste of the food. Hence, the mind never enjoys the material world: it enjoys its shadow (relayed vibrations). It is the body that enjoys material world.

Effects of the Environment and Food

A human being's physical body consists of many trillions of cells. Each of these cells has its own individual unit mind and soul. The unit mind of each of these cells is different from that of the human being. But our unit mind is affected by all the unit minds of the cells. The unit mind of each cell is undeveloped, and later, in the evolution process, each of these unit cell minds will develop into a human mind.

Most cells of the human body live for about three weeks and then die. The body generates new cells to replace the old ones. We discard these old cells when we take a bath, rub our skin, and so on.

We acquire the basis of our cells from the food we eat and the environment. Therefore, we should choose proper food and a proper environment, as cells affect our mind and, in turn, all our propensities.

Food is divided into three categories: sentient, mutative, and static. Sentient food produces sentient cells, causing physical and mental well-being. Examples of sentient foods are fruits, rice, barley, legumes, rice, and milk. Mutative food produces mutative cells, which are good for the body and may or may not good for the mind; they are not harmful for the mind. Examples of mutative foods are red chili, and caffeinated tea and coffee. Static food may or may not be good for body but are certainly harmful for mind. Examples of static food are wine, meat, fish, eggs, onions, and garlic.

7

•◆•

KARMA AND POTENTIAL ENERGY

I was born in a village. My father was a teacher in the city. When I was a child, we used to go to our village in a bullock cart from the nearest railway station, twenty miles from the village. At that time, there was no electricity in the village. But now they have all the modern gadgets. One very poor farm laborer used to tell my father that if he would see God, he would cut his throat with a knife, because he made him poor. But we will see in this chapter that God gives equal opportunity to everyone, and it is up to the person to write his or her own fate, and the entire universe is an ordered system operated by the cosmic operative principle (the force of creation).

Present Unanswered Questions

We see the following incidents every day, and the majority of religions cannot explain them properly.

1. Why do good things happen to a bad person and bad things happen to a good person?

2. Even if you are a good driver and are driving safely, somebody hits your car and injures you.

3. On August 1, 2007, when the eight-lane I-35W Mississippi River bridge in Minneapolis, Minnesota, catastrophically failed during the evening rush hour, several automobiles went into the river, killing 13 people and injuring 145. Several vehicles remained hanging on the top of the collapsed bridge span. People inside the hanging vehicles survived. Was it just by chance that people who died were unlucky and were got killed?

4. In earthquakes, volcanic eruptions, or tsunamis, scores of people die, yet a few are found alive in the debris, even after several days after the catastrophic events.

5. How did you come to this world: in your mother's womb, in a particular family, a particular geographical area?

6. Recent genetic breakthroughs have revealed that certain types of people are predisposed to certain diseases. What is the reason behind it?

We could list many more incidents present-day religions cannot explain satisfactorily. As discussed in the previous chapters, founders of today's religions were great persons of their times. They preached to their disciples according to the culture and knowledge prevalent in their times. But because of the advancement of science and technology, these religions are now out of date.

Judgment Day

In many religions, there is a concept of "Last Judgment" or "Judgment Day." It will take place after the resurrection of the dead. God will preside over it and will give the Final Judgment (that is, who will go to Heaven and who will go to Hell) to all, depending on their deeds. For this very reason, they started the practice of preserving the dead bodies so that they can rise on Judgment Day.

A couple of thousand years ago, when science was not developed as much as today, the founders of religions said there would be a Judgment Day, and on that day, God would punish and reward everyone according to their deeds. They did so because it was not possible for them to explain things according to science as then known.

The problem is, who is writing or keeping track of each and every second of each and every person? After all, there are billions of people on Earth as well as trillions and trillions of people-like creatures on trillions and trillions of Earth-like planets in the multi-universe.

Also, if they are correct, there has to be "something" within a human body that leaves the body after death and waits until Judgment Day. This "something" cannot live inside the dead body until Judgment Day, as per their assumptions, because scores of dead bodies are vaporized by incidents like volcanic eruptions and bombings of graveyards during wars. In two space shuttle disasters (*Challenger* in 1986 and *Columbia* in 2003), fourteen brave astronauts lost their lives, and their complete bodies were not found. Therefore, there is nothing within our body that lives until Judgment Day.

There has to be "something" inside our body that leaves it once we are dead.

Recycling and Billions of Years of History of Everything in the Universe

In the universe, nothing disappears suddenly. Everything is recycled. For example, whatever water we get during rain is recycled. Rainwater is usually evaporated water from ocean or river. It either goes underground, turning into groundwater, or is used by humans before it finally goes into rivers or oceans via drainage. This water may also be recycled into some other form. We can change this water into some other material through chemical reactions. This is true with all the things we see around us.

Everything we see around us has billions of years of history. You may say you bought a brand-new television, but each and every part constituting the television has its own history to tell and can be traced to their manufacturing firms. The manufacturing firms bought minerals from mines to manufacture the parts that make up the television. The mining firms dug minerals from the earth. The minerals were formed when materials went through millions of years of transformation underground. It is also true with a brand-new wood table you buy in a store. The wood making up the table came from a tree that grew in the soil. This soil was formed from something else, and so on. In this way, one can trace the history of everything around us back billions of years. This is also true with the human souls, as they are also recycled.

In prehistoric times, people who had no knowledge about the existence of rivers and oceans or how the rain is formed might have claimed some god created rain and clouds out of nothing so that they would get water. Religions, which claim humans are specially created by God, are nothing but like prehistoric people, who might have claimed the creation of rain clouds by some god out of nothing.

Science and Technology

Here are some facts about science.

1. If somebody had created electricity or television in the ninth century, people would have regarded that person as a god and thought he had captured the sun and kept the accounts of what others had done previously. It would not have been possible to explain these phenomena by the science prevalent at that time.

2. Four or five hundred years ago, if somebody claimed he had data about all the people on Earth on a tiny flash drive and could track each and every one at any time by GPS, or access the life history of any person with just a keystroke, no one would have believed him.

3. If you temporarily dump some highly radioactive waste near an area occupied by people still living in the Stone Age in Andaman and Nicobar Islands (a part of India), in the Bay of Bengal, they will start to die in a very short time from cancer once they come in contact with the radioactive waste. Because they do not know anything about radioactivity, they will consider it God's curse.

As discussed in chapter 4, our universe is billions (maybe trillions) of years old, whereas, our present-day science is just two hundred to three hundred years old. Therefore, present-day science has just started to scratch the surface of the scientific laws of the universe and may not have knowledge of maybe millions of scientific laws of universe (the cosmic operative principle).

Over the last ten thousand years, saints in Asia have developed Tantra. They have come up with the concept of karma, also called reactive momenta. Karma is somewhat comparable to the potential energy in our science. We discuss karma in this chapter.

Energy Definitions

When you go to Niagara Falls, you see the beautiful water dropping from such a great height. If a person with scientific background goes there, he or she may think that water has potential energy on top, which is converted into kinetic energy at the bottom. The kinetic energy can be converted into electricity. For this very reason, there is an electrical plant near Niagara Falls.

Suppose you pick up a book from the floor and place it on a table. Then, the book "gains" a potential energy of mgh, where

m = mass of book
g = gravitational constant (a constant number)
h = height of table

You do not calculate this potential energy and add it to the book, but there is a built-in mechanism in the universe that adds this potential energy to the book. This book has a "potential" to drop by "h" height, so this energy is called potential energy. In layperson's terms, potential energy can be likened to squeezing a ball. The ball will always have a tendency to regain its original shape. This tendency is its potential energy.

Similarly, we have energies like chemical energy and nuclear energy. Five hundred years ago, nobody thought chemical, electrical, or nuclear energy existed and in future, new energies can be conceptualized and discovered. To explain physical phenomenon, science came up with these energy terminologies.

Transformation of Energies by Our Actions

Each and every second, we inadvertently use perhaps hundreds of scientific laws of the cosmic operative principle. We are also transforming several types of energies to other forms. For example, when you clap, you use two hands, one clashing against the other. In this process, the two hands create pressure on each other, and through certain mechanisms, this pressure is felt in your brain. Inside your palm, one cell relays the message of pressure to another cell via electrochemical energy transformation and so on. There may be billions and trillions of physical cells that take part in conveying the message of pressure from your palm to your brain. All these cells go through energy transformations to convey this message.

Clapping also generates heat. So, a feeling of heat is also conveyed to the brain through some chemical process (electrochemical energy transformation) and finally to your mind by nerve cells. Again, the number of physical cells involved may be billions and trillions. Heat also travels via air particles in the form of heat vibrations and is relayed to your entire body, although the amount of heat is very minute.

Clapping generates sound, too. This sound travels through air by displacing the air particles near your palms. One air particle relays the sound vibration to another air particle. Finally, this sound vibration strikes your ear canal, from where it is relayed to your brain by your nerve cells and then to your mind. Again, the number of physical cells involved in this process may be billions and trillions. Sound travels through your skin, too. Here again, your trillions of physical cells go through different types of energy transformations to convey this sound message to your brain.

Your bones and the muscles in your palms feel pressure during the clapping, and these involve several types of energy transformations. And when you clap, people nearby also feel it. All the above-mentioned vibrations also strike their sensory organs. Hence, their physical cells go through many of the same energy transformations as yours.

We see that just a simple clapping triggers so many scientific laws of universe (cosmic operative principle), which we never really consider. Similarly, if you inhale, exhale, walk, talk, or even sleep, you inadvertently use hundreds or even thousands of scientific laws of the universe and transform numerous types of energies from one form to another.

Karma (Reactive Momenta)

The mind is never stable. Its focus changes from time to time—in most cases, without one's control. If a student is thinking about a house right now, within seconds, the subject may change to homework; after some seconds, the subject may change to movies, and so on. Sometimes in class, and despite one's best efforts, one cannot concentrate on the lecture. This shows the mind is not within one's control but guided by some other force.

According to Newton's First Law of Motion, there has to be a force in order to change the static or dynamic state of a particle. In short, a table cannot move or change its position without the application of a force. As a change of subject is always mental, there has to be a subtle force within us that causes a frequent change of the subject in the mind.

The mind's change of subject, or mental fluctuation, is due to karma (reactive momenta). Whatever deeds—bad or good—one has done in this or past lives are stored in the soul. These accumulated potential energies within oneself are the causes of mental fluctuation.

If you jump from a table, it does not hurt too much. If you jump from a one-story building, you may break a leg. If you jump from a thirty-story building, you will be dead. This happens because of immediate reaction given by the earth. With whatever force you will jump on the earth, it will hurt you back with the same intensity. If you jump from a table, you are not jumping on the earth with a large force, so it will not hurt you as much. When you jump from a thirty-story building, you come down on the earth with a large force, and it will hit you back with the same amount of force. This tells us there is a built-in system in this universe that always gives an equal and opposite reaction to every action.

According to the theory of karma, whatever you do, think, or speak is subject to a built-in mechanism in the universe. The cosmic operative principle attaches a karma to your unit mind so that you will reap accordingly. If you hurt someone, you actually hurt yourself, as you must reap whatever you have done. The force of this universe/cosmic operative principle is not going to leave you, although it may take time before it hits.

Every religion says that one day we will have to reap whatever we do. Apart from this, the majority of religions say God is watching all of us every second. The theory of karma confirms those ideas. The theory of karma conforms to the three requirements of a scientific theory:

1. The theory of karma is universal. It is applicable everywhere—for anyone on Earth and for humanlike creatures on similar planets in the universe.
2. The theory of karma is not time dependent. It is applicable today, millions of years from now, and was applicable millions of years in the past.
3. The theory of karma is not space dependent. It is applicable everywhere in the multi-universe.

One important feature of the theory of karma is that unlike several religions, it does not divide human society. Therefore, one should not fear anyone except oneself, as no one can write his karma except himself or herself. The individual alone can do good or bad to reap good or bad karma.

The difference between an animal and a human is that whatever an animal does is according to the rules of the cosmic operative principle or its inborn instinct/physical needs. What a human does is according to intellect as well as intuition, and the person has to bear the fruits in the form of karma.

One day, you will have to bear the fruits of your karma. While reaping the fruits of one of your previous acts, you are not acting independently. In such a case, the force of the cosmic operative principle will make you to do it. The negative karma will bring mental pain, disgrace, and accusations.

When a good person does a bad act due to karma, he or she feels sad and regrets about actions; a bad person enjoys it. Using fMRI, researchers at the University of Chicago have found bullies actually enjoy the pain they cause others. The part of the brain associated with reward lights up when an aggressive teen watches a video of someone hurting another person, but not when a nonaggressive youth watches the same clip.[37]

If you commit a crime or good work, you may not reap its fruits immediately or in the same manner. You may get the fruits of your action(s) in a circular way, involving several people. The water, which evaporates and becomes rain clouds, does not rain in the same place. Similarly, dust in your house may be from the next city, the planet Saturn, or from some other solar system.

Karma can be both positive and negative. For a devotee, both types of karma are bad. To him or her, a chain is a chain, be it a gold chain or an iron chain. Unless a soul gets rid of all its karma, the soul cannot get salvation. If a devotee surrenders all his actions to the Supreme Consciousness, the person will not get any karma.

Revenge

If somebody breaks your leg, you need to file a case against him with the police. Filing a case against him with police is considered an appropriate action. But if you also break that person's leg, it is called revenge, and legally, you are as eligible for punishment as much as he or she is.

The law of universe works in the same way. If you take revenge, you, too, are eligible for punishment by the law of universe. It is the duty of Mother Nature/universe—not you—to punish the perpetrator. For this purpose, you do not have to plead with anyone, because the moment one conducts a crime, an appropriate (negative) karma is attached to his or her soul. But to maintain law and order in the materialistic word, one has to report a crime to the police. Otherwise, if everyone leaves it to Mother Nature to take appropriate action against the perpetrator, criminals would rule the world.

After Death

Once a person dies, all of his or her mind, along with its karma, leaves the body. Almost all of his or her memories, and all physical nerve cells, become one with the earth. But some of his memories, called extracerebral memories, are attached to the departing mind. These noncerebral memories correspond to the karmas that did not bear fruits in the previous lives, as well as to the episodes in which the individual and his or her mind were deeply involved. These memories do not last long once a person is born. With most people, the extracerebral memory gradually fades away after the age of five. It would be difficult for one to remember his or her past life, as the individual may develop a dual personality. But sometimes, the person may suddenly imagine something that seems like déjà vu: for example, "I have seen this old building before." The individual says this without knowing these are events from past lives.

Here, I want to give an example of the selection of the Dalai Lama (and also other high lamas). After the death of the Dalai Lama, his disciples search for his reincarnation in Tibet and nearby areas based on the visions in the dreams of high lamas. Once they find a boy believed to be the reincarnation of the departed lama, they conduct a series of tests on him. They present him with the belongings of the previous Dalai Lama, along with several other objects. If the boy chooses the belongings of the previous Dalai Lama instead of other objects, and they get some other indications, the disciples declare the boy to be the reincarnation of the previous Dalai Lama. Among Tibetan Buddhists, Panchen Lama is the second-highest authority, after Dalai Lama. A six-year-old boy named Gedhun Choekyi Nyima was selected as the reincarnation of the tenth Panchen Lama, that is, as the eleventh Panchen Lama, in 1995. But the Chinese government took him into custody immediately after he was declared the eleventh Panchen Lama and named another boy, Gyaincain Norbu, as the eleventh Panchen Lama. Gedhun Choekyi Nyima is still in the custody of the Chinese government.

After a person's death, his or her mind and unspent karma and noncerebral memories leave the body and move around in the universe until, with the help of the cosmic operative principle, it finds an appropriate body. The new body will be that of a plant, animal, human, and so on, based on its karma. It moves around invisibly and inaudibly. Hence, it is not possible for anyone to see or hear it. But by giving a part of the person's own ectoplasmic stuff, a tantrika can help this mind get a temporary ectoplasmic body and even become temporarily visible and audible. There are two types of tantrikas: Vidya Tantrika and Avidya Tantrika. Vidya Tantrika works for the person's salvation and the welfare of the universe. Avidya Tantrika works for material gains. During the 1970s, there was an accountant in our neighborhood in our town in India. His son was my best friend. People would pay him to talk to their dead relatives.

One can explain all the unanswered questions in the beginning of this chapter on the basis of the karma theory.

As discussed previously, karma is not necessarily consummated immediately. An object's potential energy requires the proper environment to realize that energy. This is true with karma also. The mind has to wait for the proper environment to satisfy its reactive momenta. Sometimes, it can achieve expression in several steps rather than in one incident. And sometimes, one karma can get its expression after several lives, as each karma needs to find proper environment to find its expression.

Like a large factory, the universe is an ordered system, operated by the cosmic operative principle. With the help of this principle, a soul takes birth where there will be the highest probability of getting the fruits of its karma. Therefore, one who knows the laws of the cosmic operative principle can tell several things about the child. People have developed several methods of making this type of prediction. Horoscope, based on the date, time, place (longitude and latitude) of birth, is one of them.

A person's mind is influenced by two types of karmas: inborn and acquired. There are two types of acquired karma: environmental and imposed. When you see some one committing crime in your neighborhood and becoming rich, you may feel like doing the same. This is the effect of environment. If someone presses you to do something—to kill someone, for example—then it is imposed karma.

In Third World countries, crime rates are generally very high compared to those in developed countries. This is because people know very few criminals are prosecuted because of corruption and lack of law and order. In rich countries or advanced countries, people think twice before committing any crime, because they know there is a high probability they will be caught. Suppose you are driving your car in a neighborhood. If you know cameras will catch you if you drive above the speed limit and automatically send a traffic ticket to your home, you are less likely to speed. Similarly, as a spiritual person knows the rule of the cosmic operative principle, he or she would not harm someone. To do so would automatically bring punishment from the cosmic operative principle. In the beginning, the spiritual person will consciously decide not to harm anyone. But later, it becomes a reflex action; that is, it will be built into the individual's mind.

The cosmic operative principle is blind: it does not leave anyone. Even if you forgive your perpetrator, the cosmic operative principle will not leave that person, and he or she will be punished. Therefore, it is better to forgive a person than to keep your mind engaged and lose mental balance by taking revenge. Why should you spend your precious time in taking revenge when you know the cosmic operative principle will not leave the perpetrator unpunished?

Moksa/Nirvana

Moksa (Nirvana or salvation) means one is liberated permanently, whereas mukti (emancipation) is temporary liberation.

The soul is the witnessing entity. According to Shrii Shrii Anandamurti ji, the soul and mind can be compared to a magnet and an iron with impurities, respectively. The soul wants salvation—to merge in non-qualified consciousness (Nirguna Brahma)—and hence, it wants the mind (the iron) to be pure to get rid of its karma, that is, impurities.

Great Spiritual Persons

It is said that Jesus Christ took our sins and suffered for us on the cross. The intensity of suffering for us will be more for the same sin than that suffered by spiritualists like Christ, Prophet Muhammad, Krishna, Buddha, and Moses. That's why it is said that a yogi does not feel pain or happiness. But in my view, he also feels pain or happiness, but not as intensely as we do.

Based on my own observations of spiritual people and spiritual stories, I have come to the conclusion that Newton's Second Law of Motion is also valid in the spiritual realm: "For the same force, a lighter particle will experience more acceleration or deceleration than a heavier particle." This can be expressed in the following notation:

$$p = mf$$

where

$$p = \text{force}$$
$$m = \text{mass}$$
$$f = \text{acceleration or deceleration}$$

In layman's terms, greater force is required to move a heavier body. and less force is required to move a smaller body.

Suppose you have $100,000, and I have only $1,000. If you give me $100,000, you will lose all your money, and I will feel like I am Bill Gates. But if Bill Gates, who has more than $50 billion, gives me the $100,000, it would be like a drop in the ocean to him.

In the spiritual sense, we may express it like this: for the same sins or good deeds, a very good person or a spiritual person will experience less pain or happiness than a bad person. Here, mass corresponds to how spiritual a person is. For this reason, almost all great spiritual persons—like Jesus, Moses, Prophet Muhammad, Krishna, Mirabai, Swami Vivekananda, and Ram Krishna Parmahansa—suffered in their lives, because they took the bad karmas of their disciples during their lifetimes out of their love for their disciples. But this transfer of karma has to be in real time and cannot be done posthumously. If I am committing sins right now, my dead spiritual teacher is not going to take my present or future bad karmas. A person has to have a human body to take my bad karma and suffer for my sins.

Before he became famous because of his lecture at the 1983 Parliament of Religions in Chicago, Swami Vivekananda sometimes did not have enough money to buy food. Because of this, he developed a number of diseases and died at age thirty-nine. Mirabai was poisoned by her own relatives. Jesus was crucified. Ram Krishna Parmahansa was a great spiritual person. He was the guru and mentor of Swami Vivekananda. Ramakrishna Parmahansa performed many miracles, not to impress people but to guide spiritual persons like Swami Vivekananda. Using the example of a monk who used to walk on water to cross the nearby river, a disciple suggested to Ramakrishna Parmahansa that he would become very famous if he could do the same. Then, Ramakrishna Parmahansa said the value of all the monk's meditation was just one anna (sixteen anna was equal to one Indian rupee), because one could cross the river on a boat by paying one anna. During his childhood, Ramakrishna Parmahansa refused to go to school, claiming he wanted to learn something that would be beneficial in all his lives and not in this life only. Hence, he remained illiterate.

Shri Shri Anandamurti ji, founder of Ananda Marga, was my spiritual teacher. He had great spiritual powers. My maternal place was Jamalpur, a small town in India, from where he also hailed. Unlike other gurus, he never allowed rich and famous persons near him. According to him, it is the obligation of every human being, rich or poor, to follow a path that leads to salvation (nirvana). Hence, he made the provision that his organization would not charge any money to teach meditation techniques. When his popularity was at its peak during the 1960s, several rich and famous persons, including senior central cabinet ministers, were initiated into his organization. But they never came to see him or attend any function of the organization, because they would not have found the special treatment they usually received elsewhere. Due to his political views, criminal cases were filed against him in the early 1970s by the Indian government, headed by Indira Gandhi, whose government depended on communist support. Shri Shri Anandamurti ji advocated a sociopolitical theory called PROUT, which was against communism. Later, the high court found all the charges baseless, and he was set free. One point worth noting is that when communists withdrew their support and Indira Gandhi was able to form a government after her party won a majority of the seats in 1980, she never uttered a negative word against Shri Shri Anandamurti ji.

During Gandhi's regime, the central investigation agency, the CBI (Central Bureau of Investigation), was known as the "Congress Bureau of Investigation," as she misused it to terrorize the opposition. Gandhi was the leader of the Congress party, which ruled from the independence of India in 1947 until 1977, when she suffered a humiliating defeat largely due to the atrocities committed during the Emergency Rule (1975–1977). In June 1975, Gandhi imposed one-party dictatorial rule and imprisoned the leaders and members of all the opposition parties. Even today, the Congress party, India's ruling party, misuses the CBI and other government agencies to intimidate the opposition, including the leaders of anticorruption movement groups fighting rampant corruption in the government.

In another high profile case against Ananda Marga, its members were charged by the CBI in connection with the assassination of L. N. Mishra, the then Railway minister. On January 2, 1975, Mishra was badly injured in a grenade attack while inaugurating a new train at Samastipur railway station in his state Bihar. The attending surgeon advised to rush Mishra to Dharbanga Medical College and Hospital (DMCH), at the time one of the four premier medical hospitals in Bihar, for surgery. The hospital was just 30 kilometers from Samastipur. However, instead Mishra, who was bleeding profusely, was brought by train to Patna, about 100 km from Samastipur. There the doctors advised that he should be rushed to Patna Medical College and Hospital (PMCH), and there again he was taken by slow train to Danapur hospital which was nowhere as compared to both DMCH and PMCH. While taking him to Danapur, the train was detained for 3 to 4 hours at a station although his train should have been given the highest priority as he was the Railway minister. Due to heavy bleeding he succumbed to death before arriving at the hospital. Hence whoever was behind the murder of L. N. Mishra made sure that he did not survive. It was alleged that Mishra was murdered by people close to Gandhi as he was building a rival power center within the party against Gandhi whose popularity was declining sharply due to large-scale corruption and record rise in the prices of food grains and other essential commodities. Mishra was the treasurer of the Congress party and he was in a position to buy party leaders. According to the Mitrokhin archive, Mishra was taking money from KGB also.[38] Mishra was a leftist and he helped Gandhi in securing crucial support from the communist party in retaining the premiership when she decided to split the ruling Congress party in 1969. Due to record rise in prices and also the rise of her son Sanjay Gandhi who was a pro-capitalist and aspired to become the Henry Ford of India by manufacturing cars, communists had started to oppose some of her policies. Although Mishra did not survive, B. N. Prasad, the then Deputy Inspector General (DIG) of police who was looking after his security, survived as he was rushed to DMCH and despite the fact that he was more seriously injured in the grenade attack than Mishra.

Immediately after the assassination of Mishra, the state police arrested one person, Arun Kumar, for the murder of Mishra. But the central government of Gandhi asked the CBI to take over the case and the CBI immediately released Arun Kumar. Instead CBI arrested and charged members of Ananda Marga for the murder of Mishra. It is worth noting that the Gandhi's own party, i.e. Congress party was governing in Bihar at that time.

Four years after CBI filed a charge-sheet against members of Ananda Marga, Supreme Court Justice V. M. Tarakunde inquired into the evidence collected by the agency and perused other documents to submit a report on February 15, 1979 at the request of then Bihar chief minister Karpoori Thakur, a non-Congress party politician. Justice Tarakunde opined for a fresh probe and release of innocent persons arrested in the case. He also reported that L. N. Mishra's widow had told D. Sen, the head of CBI, that she suspected Bihar politician Ram Bilas Jha for her husband's murder and was told by Sen not to go public with this as it would lead to "higher ups." After the CBI declined the fresh probe and release of the accused Ananda Marga members, Justice Tarakunde directed the CBI for day-to-day trial in the L. N. Mishra murder case.[39] Within few weeks of assassination of Mishra in 1975, the then chief minister of Bihar state, Abdul Gafoor was replaced by the Jagannath Mishra, the brother of L. N. Mishra, to quell the anger of Brahmins, of which L. N. Mishra belonged to and also a vote bank of Congress party.

Still today after 37 years of the assassination of L. N. Mishra, a very senior minister and influential political leader, the CBI has not conducted the trial even in a lower court. In December 2011, a two member bench of Supreme Court, comprising of Justices H. L. Dattu and C. K. Prasad, issued notice to CBI on why the case had dragged on for so long. Of the 39 defense witnesses cited by one accused to prove his innocence, 31 have died. [40]

My family was very close to Shri Shri Anandamurti ji. We had a chance to witness his spiritual powers, which cannot be explained by our present-day science. He showed events on the wall, like movies, to hundreds of people about what they did in their present lives. Devashish Donald Acosta published a book (*Anandamurti: The Jamalpur Years*, 2010) about Jamalpur years of Shri Shri Anandamurti ji. In the book, there is narration of about two hundred incidents/miracles relating to approximately two hundred fifty people. There are also some stories in the book about my family. My family knew all these people. Several people mentioned in the book are still alive, and therefore these stories can be verified.

A liberated soul does not have any karma of its own as the soul is liberated from the cycle of birth and rebirth. Therefore, if it wants to be born on Earth to guide humanity on a spiritual path, the soul has to acquire karma. The soul will not acquire karma of a wealthy person (or good karmas). Instead, the soul would opt for bad karmas of spiritual persons (still born on Earth) to take birth so that they (spiritual persons) get salvation quickly. For this very reason, the souls who have already been liberated from the cycle of birth and rebirth suffer on Earth, not because of their karmas, but because of others' karmas. These great souls take birth on planets like Earth to show people like us the spiritual path as well as explain spirituality according to the prevalent science and culture.

In my view, great persons like Christ, Buddha, and Krishna knew laws of the universe (cosmic operative principle) we do not know. That is why we claim their works are miracles, magic, or religious dogma. Mental or spiritual science may someday show none of these characterizations is correct and that these teachers were putting deep scientific principles into play. Also, these great spiritual persons, as well as others who have progressed on a spiritual path, can read our hard drive (in the brain as well as in the mind) by sending subtle waves. Hence, they can tell our past and predict our future.

God—No God

Toward the end of Buddha's life, one of his disciples asked him about the existence of God. He was asked two questions: "Does God exist?" and, "Is it a fact that God does not exist?" Buddha did not reply to either of the questions and kept silent. For this very reason, there are three interpretations of God in Buddhism: (1) one section interpreted Buddha's silence to mean that God exists; (2) a second section interpreted his silence to mean that God does not exist; and (3) the third section interpreted his silence to mean that God's existence is inexplicable.

In Tantra, there is a concept of Taraka Brahma, who resides within the scope of nonqualified consciousness (Nirguńa Brahma) and qualified consciousness (Saguńa Brahma), but along the tangential touch of both. It is up to the person who reaches the ultimate destiny in spirituality (that is, salvation) to either merge in the non-qualified consciousness or get out of qualified consciousness by a tangential touch to the abode of Taraka Brahma. Taraka Brahma knows everything about the cosmic operative principle, nonqualified consciousness, and qualified consciousness.

Final Words

Nuclear fusion and fission are well-known occurrences. But no one can produce an atomic bomb or electricity from nuclear processes simply by obtaining radioactive material. A sophisticated lab and knowledge of the proper techniques are required. Similarly, for mental development, utilization, and control, a person has to go to a good teacher and learn to do research work (meditation) in the laboratory of the mind.

If one can find a good tantrik teacher, it is very easy to acquire some spiritual/tantrik powers, such as to know what a person has done in the past or what is going to happen to someone in the immediate future. But I would not regard him as a good spiritual person. A great person is one who uses spiritual powers not only for his or her own spiritual development but also to guide others for the welfare (spiritual, social, economic, political, and so on) of the human society rather than to make money.

ENDNOTES

• ◆ •

Chapter 4

1 "Star survey reaches 70 sextillion," *CNN.com*, July 22, 2003.
2 Borenstein, Seth, "Cosmic census finds crowd of planets in our galaxy," *AP*, February 19, 2011.
3 Alleyne, Richard, "AAAS: 'One hundred billion trillion' planets where alien life could flourish," *Telegraph* (UK), February 15, 2009.
4 Moskowitz, Clara, "Star Trek's warp drive: Not impossible," *Space.com*, May 6, 2009.
5 Roach, John, "Unknown 'structures' tugging at universe, study says," *National Geographical News*, November 5, 2008.
6 Ibid.
7 Randerson, James, "One big bang, or were there many?" *Guardian* (UK), May 5, 2006.
8 Hinshaw, Gary F., "What is the universe made of?" Universe 101, map.gsfc.nasa.gov/universe/uni_matter.html, January 29, 2010.

9   Zwicky, F., "On the Masses of Nebulae and of Clusters of Nebulae," *Astrophysical Journal*, 1937, vol. 86, p.217.

10   Connor, Steve, "The universe gives up its deepest secret," *Independent* (UK), January 8, 2007.

Chapter 5

11   "Humpback whales have 'human' brain cells: Study," *Reuters,* November 27, 2006; Linden, Eugene, "Can Animals Think?" *Time,* March 22, 1993.

12   Lloyd, Robin, "Like Humans, Other Apes Plan Ahead," *LiveScience.com*, June 17, 2008.

13   "Birds can distinguish languages: Researchers," *AFP,* February 2, 2006.

14   Begley, Sharon, "In our messy, reptilian brains," *Newsweek,* April 9, 2007.

15   Jonsson, Patrik, "New research opens a window on the minds of plants," *abcnews.com,* March 3, 2005.

16   Schmid, Randolph E., "Stressed plants produce an aspirin-like chemical," *AP,* September 18, 2008.

17   Pelvig, D. P., Pakkenberg, H., Stark, A.K., Pakkenberg, B., "Neocortical glial cell numbers in human brains," *Neurobiology of Aging* 29 (11), 2008, pp. 1754–1762.

18   Drachman D, "Do we have brain to spare?," *Neurology* 64 (12), 2005, pp. 2004–5.

19   "Single brain cell's power shown," *BBC News,* December 22, 2007.

20   Witelson, S.F., Kigar, D.L. and Harvey, T., "The Exceptional Brain of Albert Einstein," *The Lancet*, vol. 353 (1999), pp. 2149-2153.

21   "Scientists find brain cells linked to choice," *Reuters,* April 23, 2006.

22 Shors, Tracey J. Shors, "How to Save New Brain Cells," *Scientific American*, February 24, 2009.

23 Laurance, Jeremy, "Scientists discover way to reverse loss of memory," *Independent* (UK), January 30, 2008.

24 Ibid.

25 Choi, Charles Q., "Why time seems to slow down in emergencies," *LiveScience.com*, December 12, 2007.

26 Beglegy, Sharon, "Experiment with wired rats gives charge to neuroscience," *Wall Street Journal*, May 2, 2002.

27 Sample, Ian, "The brain scan that can read people's intentions," *Guardian*, February 9, 2007.

Chapter 6

28 Shrii Shrii Anandamurti, "Acoustic Roots," *Ananda Vacanamrtam Part 14*, AMPS.

29 Angier, Natalie, "Sorry, Vegans: Brussels Sprouts Like to Live, Too," *The New York Times*, December 24, 2009.

30 Shrii Shrii Anandamurti, *Yoga Psychology*, 3rd ed., 1998, AMPS, p. 158.

31 Ibid., pp. 138–144.

32 Ibid., p. 159.

33 Shrii Shrii Anandamurti, *Discourses on Krsna and the Giita*, AMPS 2004, pp. 191–192.

34 "Meditation 'brain training' clues," *BBC News*, June 13, 2005.

35 "Meditation shown to light up brains of Buddists," *Reuters*, May 21, 2003.

36 Shrii Shrii Anandamurti, "Acoustic Roots," *A'nanda Vacana'mrtam Part 14*, AMPS.

Chapter 7

37 "Brain scans show bullies enjoy others' pain," *Washingtonpost.com*, November 7, 2008.

38 Andrew, Christopher and Mitrokhin, Vasili, *The World Was Going Our Way: The KGB and The Battle for the Third World*, Basic Books, 2005, p. 322.

39 Mahapatra, Dhananjay, "SC: Why has LN Mishra murder trial dragged for 37 years?," *The Times of India*, December 16, 2011.

40 Ibid.

CPSIA information can be obtained at www.ICGtesting.com
Printed in the USA
LVOW111748090512

281059LV00016B/119/P